Mountain Ministry
Living on Grace Street

Kenneth K. Humphreys

Parson's Porch Books

Mountain Ministry: Living on Grace Street
ISBN 978-1-949888-34-8
Copyright © 2017 by Kenneth K. Humphreys

All rights reserved. No part of this book may be reproduced or transmitted in any form or by any means, electronic or mechanical, including photocopying, recording, or by any information storage and retrieval system, without permission in writing from the publisher.

All scripture quotations, except as otherwise noted in the text, are taken from the Holy Bible, New International Version® NIV®
Copyright ©1973, 1978, 1984, 2011 by Biblica, Inc. ®
Used by permission. All rights reserved worldwide.

The "NIV" and "New International Version' are trademarks registered in the United States Patent and Trademark Office by Biblica, Inc.®

Photo Credits: Martha Childers Jordan, photo on cover of the author sitting with Hunter Ray and her parents, Monica and Daniel Ray: The author, photos on the back of Siloam Presbyterian Church, Old Fort, NC and Conley Memorial Presbyterian Church, Marion, NC

To order additional copies of the book, contact:

Parson's Porch Books
1-423-475-7308
www.parsonsporch.com

Parson's Porch is an imprint of Parson's Porch & Company (PP&C) in Cleveland, Tennessee. PP&C is an innovative organization which raises money by publishing books of noted authors, representing all genres. All donations from contributions and profits are shared with the poor.

*Mountain Ministry
Living on Grace Street*

Contents

Foreword by Rev. Edyth Potter Pruitt   **11**
Preface   13

PART ONE

Sermons for Major Sundays of the Christian Year

Christmas, Advent, Epiphany, Baptism of the Lord, Transfiguration of the Lord, Lent, Easter, Pentecost, Trinity Sunday, Stewardship Sunday, and Christ the King Sunday

Seeing God in the Face of a Child   19
(A Christmas or baptismal sermon)
Luke 2:22-40

A Conflicted Time of Year   22
(An Advent sermon)
Psalm 25; 1 Thessalonians 3:9-13; Luke 21:25-36

You Can't Buy God's Grace   26
 (A sermon for Epiphany or Baptism of the Lord Sunday)
Luke 3:15-17, 21-22; Acts 8:14- 23

Returning to the Mountain   29
(A sermon for Transfiguration of the Lord Sunday)
2 Kings 2:1-12; 2 Corinthians 4:3-6; Mark 9:2-9

Living on Grace Street   32
(A sermon for Lent)
1 Peter 3:18-22

Justification by Grace   36
(A sermon for Easter Sunday)
Acts 10:34-43; 1 Corinthians 15:1-11

A Divine Gift   41
(A sermon for Pentecost)
John 14:8-17, 25-27

Three Gods or One?   44
(A sermon for Trinity Sunday)
Isaiah 6:1-8; John 3:1-17

It's a Puzzlement   48
(A sermon for Trinity Sunday)
Romans 5:1-5; John 16:12-15

She Gave All That She Had   51
(A stewardship sermon)
Mark 12:38-44

King for All Eternity   55
(A sermon for Christ the King Sunday)
Psalm 132; Revelation 1:4b-8; John 18:33-37

PART TWO:

Sermons for Other Sundays of the Christian Year
(Ordinary Time)

The Wisdom of Children   61
James 3:13-4:3, 7-8a: Mark 9:30-37

Talking to Children   65
Mark 9:30-37

Give Thanks: Surrender to the Grace of God   68
Mark 13:1-8

Living a Servant Life   72
Ruth 1:1-18

Watching and Waiting   75
Matthew 25:14-30

Our God of Love   79
Romans 10:8b-14

The Greatest Commandment   83
Matthew 22:34-46

Why Are We Afraid of Evangelism?   87
Isaiah 60:1-5a; Acts 9:1-19

Don't Pull the Weeds   91
Matthew 13:24-30, 36-43

Living Water   95
Exodus 17:1-7; John 4:5-42

The First Will Be Last, and the Last Will Be First   98
Mark 10:17-31

Applying for a Job Following Jesus   102
Mark 10:17-31, 46-52

Blind Ambition   106
Mark 10:35-45

The Heavens Declare the Glory of God   110
Psalm 19

Poor in the World, Rich in Faith   114
James 2:1-17

Thousands More Commandments   118
Mark 7:1-8, 14-15, 21-23

613 Commandments   121
Acts 10:1-16

Pray for Everyone   125
1 Timothy 2:1-7

Centering Your Life   129
Jeremiah 18:1-11; Luke 14:2

Do You Understand What You Pray for?   131
Matthew 6:5-15; Luke 11:1-13

Will God Answer Your Prayers?   135
Luke 11:1-13

Women's Lib in Judea   139
Luke 10:38-42

The Bay of Pigs   140
Galatians 3:23-29; Luke 8:26-39

A Story of Two Sinners   143
Luke 7:36-50

We Are Number One, or Are We?   145
Mark 10:35-45

Mom and Dad Know Best --- or Do They?   149
Acts 11:1-18

Turning 180 Degrees   152
Acts 10:34-48

A Basket Case   156
Acts 9:19b-31

God Speaks to Everyone   160
Acts 11:1-18

Table Fellowship   164
Luke 15:1-10

Get Up!   163
Acts 9:32-43

Insurmountable Odds   167
1 Samuel 17: 4-49

A House Divided   171
Mark 3:20-25

Seeing: The Last Miracle   **180**
Mark 10:46-52

Don't Overestimate Yourself   **183**
Mark 9:38-50

Foreword

Back in 1989, I had the privilege of being called to the mission field to work with Youth For Christ in Namibia, South West Africa. As I packed my bags to go, my father gave me wise words, "Remember who you are and where you come from". Those words resonated with me over and over as I faced a world very different than the world I knew as a child. Those words grounded me and reminded me that no matter what I faced in the world, I had been equipped for the moments that I would face a world away from family and friends. This grounding enabled me to see family and friends in the wider circle of life as I remembered who I was, as a child of God and where I came from, as a participant in the long line of believers from all times and places. All along my journey, I was the recipient of gentle reminders of the love that had formed me, the community that had prepared me, and the grace that would sustain me for the calling to which disciples of Jesus Christ have been called. In my journey, I was reminded over and over again that no matter where we go, grace goes before us and God is ready to meet us no matter where we are. It is the gentle reminders of God's calling and grace that equip us for the journey we face, no matter where we are called.

In our current time, it sometimes seems like we, as the Christian community, are living in a foreign land, and in fact, we are! Even in the mountains of North Carolina, where there is a church on every corner, the plethora of information in this internet age crowds our minds with competing voices which seem to pull us further away from the truth of "who we are and where we come from". One of the tasks of the preacher in this confusing time is to bring us back to the center of God --- the grace we find in the gospel of Jesus Christ. In this collection of sermons, Ken Humphreys does just that. He reminds us that we are held by God, redeemed by Christ, claimed by love and have a home on "Grace Street" no matter where life may take us. This book contains gentle reminders of God's call upon our lives and equips us all --- whether raised in the church community or not --- to embrace our identity as children of God and inspires us to live into the calling to which we have been called. In its pages, you will find whispers of hope which inspires the church to seek new vistas, reminders of love in action which call us to participation in God's grand plan for our world, and the timeless truth of God's presence with us in our own communities challenging us to live vibrant lives of faith for our time.

Edyth Potter Pruitt, Pastor
Fairview Presbyterian Church
Lenoir, NC
October 2016

Preface

When I retired from engineering, no one could have told me that I would enter the ministry. I had considered becoming a pastor many years earlier but dismissed the idea as being impractical. I had a wife and four small children to support and couldn't see how I could possibly take off the requisite amount of time to study for the ministry, so I continued to work as an engineer, eventually earning a Doctor of Engineering Management degree.

I worked as an engineer in Chicago, Pittsburgh, and Morgantown, WV where I served as a professor at West Virginia University and later as Executive Director of my professional society, the American Association of Cost Engineers (AACE International).

I took early retirement in 1993 and my wife Betsy and I moved to Granite Falls, North Carolina where we became very active members of the Waldensian Presbyterian Church in Valdese, NC, and later the Fairview Presbyterian Church in Lenoir, NC.

While at Fairview I learned about a program of the Presbytery of Western North Carolina to educate lay people to better serve Christ and I enrolled in the program. At that point, I had no intention to become a pastor, but I could feel God's call, and I resisted it.

The Presbytery's program consisted of two years of classes on alternate Saturdays. The classes covered, among many other things, preaching, and I got hooked. I couldn't deny God's call any longer. I went well beyond the requirements of the program, then called the "School of the Laity", and purchased every book mentioned by the instructors, even casually, and voraciously read them.

I finished the program in December 2009 and only as few weeks later began serving as interim supply pastor along with another graduate of the program at my home church, Fairview Presbyterian, while the pastor, Rev. Edyth Pruitt was on a three-month sabbatical.

After that I did pulpit supply at a number of churches, one of which was First Presbyterian in Bessemer City, NC where I was called as co-pastor, serving there for a bit over one year.

First Presbyterian really was too small to support two pastors so I left there and resumed work as a supply preacher once again. One of the churches I went to was Conley Memorial Presbyterian near Marion, NC. I went there in January 2012 supposedly for only four weeks. After those four weeks I was called as their pastor.

Conley Memorial is a very small church which holds services at 9:30 AM each Sunday rather than the traditional time of 11:00 AM. Because of that it didn't take long for other pastors in the area to realize that I might be able to preach for them at 11:00 AM and soon I was once again doing pulpit supply, this time in addition to serving Conley Memorial as their pastor --- double duty virtually every Sunday, often driving many miles through the mountains between services.

One of the churches I went to was Siloam Presbyterian near Old Fort, NC. Siloam is about twenty miles from Conley Memorial which is close enough for me to easily get to after the 9:30 AM service at Conley Memorial each Sunday. Just as had happened at Conley Memorial, after a few weeks Siloam called me as their pastor. Now I had two churches to serve. Siloam is a tiny seasonal church which holds services from Easter Sunday through World Communion Sunday in October so, guess what, from October until Easter I do pulpit supply.

Time flies when one is having fun they say, and it is fun for me to serve the Lord in this way. Neither church is large enough to be able to financially afford to call a regular pastor, far from it, so I serve quite literally as a labor of love, not for any significant income. I can't think of a better way for a retiree to serve God than this.

The sermons in this book were preached at Conley Memorial or both Conley Memorial and Siloam. Some of them were preached at other churches including Trinity Presbyterian in Prescott, AZ where our daughter Karen Brown is on staff.

I am grateful to the good folks at Conley Memorial and Siloam Presbyterian Churches for their love and support. Most of all I am grateful and thankful for the support on my wife Betsy who I met at the Bellefield Presbyterian Church in Pittsburgh when both of us were students at Carnegie Institute of Technology (now Carnegie Mellon University). Betsy still attends our home church of Fairview Presbyterian and assists in teaching their adult Bible study class. She does go with me the 110-mile around trip to my two churches about once a month and sits through the same sermon twice. It is to her that I dedicate this book.

Part One

Sermons for Major Sundays of the Christian Year

(Christmas, Advent, Epiphany, Baptism of the Lord,
Transfiguration of the Lord, Lent, Easter, Pentecost,
Trinity Sunday, Stewardship Sunday, and
Christ the King Sunday)

Seeing God in the Face of a Child
(A Christmas or baptismal sermon)
Luke 2:22-40

Our scripture passage describes how Mary and Joseph presented their newborn son, Jesus, at the temple in accordance with Jewish custom. As I read it, I couldn't help but think of our custom today for parents to present their infant children for baptism in the church.

When parents today bring their children for baptism, they are presenting their children to God and are pledging to teach the faith to their children and to dedicate them to Christ. That may seem a bit farfetched to some people but it really isn't.

The baptismal ceremony often includes the words:

"O Lord, uphold this child by your Holy Spirit. Give this child the spirit of wisdom and understanding, the spirit of counsel and might, the spirit of knowledge and the fear of the Lord, the spirit of joy in your presence, both now and forever".

And directly addressing the child, the pastor says, *"Child of the covenant, you have been sealed by the Holy Spirit in baptism, and marked as Christ's own forever."*

Marked as Christ's own forever! The child is being given to God. Did you ever think about that?

Does God ever acknowledge that gift?

In my mind, most certainly. I can see God in the face of each child at baptism. Without question, I certainly saw God in the face of our grandson Emmett when I baptized him. We present our children for baptism and God is certainly present when we do.

When the infant Jesus was presented at the temple, he wasn't baptized then but he was presented to God in much the same manner.

According to Jewish custom newborn children were sacred to God. First born sons were presented to God in the temple and the parents offered a lamb or a pigeon as a burnt offering and a pigeon as a sin offering. Those who could afford it would offer the lamb as the burnt offering. The poor would offer the pigeon as Mary and Joseph did.

When they presented Jesus to the Lord and offered their sacrifice something happened which was quite different than what was expected. Two prophets, Simeon and Anna were in the temple and witnessed what was happening and both of them saw God in the face of the infant Jesus.

Simeon was very old and devout and had been assured by the Holy Spirit that he would not die until he had seen the Christ, the Messiah. He went to the temple that day guided by the Holy Spirit at the very hour when Jesus was being presented. He held the Christ Child and saw God in his face. He saw the consolation of Israel, the beginning of the Messianic age. He saw Jesus as the means by which all will be saved, both Jews and gentiles.

But, Simeon saw that this salvation would not come easily. He saw, in the words of William Barclay [1], *"It (will be) the hand of Jesus which lifts a man out of shame into glory"* but *"He will meet much opposition. Towards Jesus Christ there can be no neutrality. We either surrender to him or we are at war with him. And it is the tragedy of life that our pride often keeps us from making that surrender which leads to victory."*

In other words, we need not to lose sight of God in the face of Jesus.

The other witness to Jesus' presentation at the temple was a prophetess named Anna. She too was very elderly. Some Bible translations suggest that she was eighty-four years of age. Others seem to say that she had been a widow for eighty-four years. Whichever it was, she was well advanced in years and had lived at the temple since her husband had died.

We don't know much about Anna except what our scripture reading tells us. According to Barclay, *"She was a widow. She had known sorrow and she had not grown bitter.*

"She spent her life in God's home with God's people. God gave us his church to be our mother in the faith. We rob ourselves of a priceless treasure when we neglect to be one with his worshipping people.

"(Anna) never ceased to pray. Public worship is great; but private worship is also great. As someone has truly said, 'They pray best together who first pray alone.' The years had left Anna without bitterness and in unshakable hope because day by day she kept contact with him who is the source of strength and in whose strength our weakness is made perfect".

Anna too saw God in the face of the infant Jesus.

Fred Craddock [2] said, *"These two aged saints are Israel in miniature, and Israel at its best: devout, obedient, constant in prayer, led by the Holy Spirit, at home in the temple, longing and hoping for the fulfillment of God's promises ... God is doing something new, but it really is not new, because hope is always joined to memory, and the new is God's keeping an old promise. As the risen Christ would later say to his disciples, 'Everything written about me in the Law of Moses and the prophets and the psalms must be fulfilled." (Luke 24:44). Anna and Simeon are a portrait of the Israel that accepted Jesus. Those who rejected him misunderstood their own tradition and therefore were not capable of recognizing him as the continuation of their own best memory and hope."*

Simeon and Anna saw the infant Jesus at the temple. Simeon had been told that he would not die until he saw the Messiah and declared, "... *my eyes have seen your salvation."* (NIV). He saw salvation in the face of a child. He saw God just as you can.

At times we may experience disappointment during the Christmas season. We may be disillusioned or sad but rise above that. Celebrate Jesus and the salvation that his birth meant for all of us. That is more than sufficient reason to celebrate no matter what other trials and travails we may experience.

Look around. Look into a child's face. Look and you will see God.

Amen.

1. William Barclay, The Gospel of Luke, rev. ed., The Westminster Press, Philadelphia, 1975
2. Fred B. Craddock, Luke: Interpretation, A Bible Commentary for Teaching and Preaching, John Knox Press, Louisville, 1973

A Conflicted Time of Year
(An Advent sermon)
Psalm 25; 1 Thessalonians 3:9-13;
Luke 21:25-36

Advent is a very conflicted time of year with the message of Advent running head on into the commercialization of Christmas.

The season of giving at Christmas and the joy of sharing is a wonderful compliment to Advent but most people long ago lost what Advent really means to the commercial Christmas culture.

As early as August in some cases stores begin to stock Christmas items on their shelves. You find ornaments, decorations, stockings and even artificial trees in supermarkets, drug stores and home supply stores like Lowes and Home Depot.

Then the day after Halloween, All Saints Day November 1, stores go into full Christmas mode with sales and displays of all kinds. The barrage of TV and newspaper ads and catalogs in the mail hit us and our towns start hanging tacky decorations on light poles everywhere.

Huge sales start earlier and earlier every year, both in stores and on-line. Black Friday has now crept into Thanksgiving Day and earlier. The crass commercialism just won't quit.

Advent is about Christ's first coming, the nativity, and his second coming, the Parousia. The merchants have come up with a parousia of a different kind, an annual one which comes earlier and earlier every year. The church has little defense against the business sector.

William H. Peterson [1] wrote, *'For all intents and purposes, then, in what has become the global culture of our societies, the culture of Christmas has effectively eclipsed the season of Advent, precluding any engagement of its primary focus, namely the manifestation of God's reign. So, then, the church needs to reclaim Advent, but 'How?' is the primary question in the face of such a massive challenge."*

In our Psalm of Lament, David again and again talks about his sinfulness and pleads with God to lead him in the right way.

We should reflect on that. I can't say that all of the hoopla about Christmas is sinful but we need to ask God to lead our minds back to the true meaning of Christmas, to the celebration of the birth of our Savior and to the expectation of the true Parousia, the time when he will return again. And before that happens there won't be months of hoopla urging us to be praying and reading our Bibles more attentively. It will just happen and we need to be prepared for it.

As Paul said in our reading from 1 Thessalonians, be thankful to God for the joy that we have in his presence. He will always be with us but Black Friday --- or Thursday --- or Wednesday won't. They are transient. God is not.

With the commercialization of Christmas, we get caught in the trap of shopping and trying to buy the "perfect" gift for everyone on our list. We worry about it. We fret over it. Why? It isn't all that important. Your friends and family will appreciate whatever you give them. Don't worry about it and get into a panic to be first in line at Wal-Mart on Black Friday every year. In truth whatever you are worrying about buying will still be available for weeks at comparable prices.

We Christians are our own worst enemies when it comes to Christmas overshadowing Advent. *"By the time Advent begins, the pressure, even from practicing Christians, to sing Christmas hymns is overwhelming (carols have already "graced" mall music for weeks). Many congregations simply surrender to the Christmas culture. [1]"*

We forget that Advent is more about the second coming than it is about the Nativity.

"Thus by the beginning of December we are well on our way to Bethlehem.

"The problem with this, of course, is that the primary focus of Advent is the full manifestation of the reign of God. This is the exclusive focus of ... Scripture readings from the Sunday after All Saints' Day until the last week of Advent. [1]" Only in the last week of Advent do we shift our focus from the second coming to the incarnation of Christ.

Advent is about the second coming, not the first. It sets the context of the entire church year. It calls us to salvation, to deeper understandings and higher expectations.

Our reading from Luke makes that abundantly clear. It speaks of Christ's return even while the earth may seem to be falling to pieces. It reminds us that *"Our worries separate us from God. We cannot prepare the way and proclaim the good news of the gospel while ensnared by the woes of the world [2]"* or by stressing over what kind of gifts to buy or what to prepare for Christmas dinner.

In his Bible paraphrase, <u>The Message</u> [3], Eugene Peterson expresses our reading from Luke this way:

25-26 "It will seem like all hell has broken loose—sun, moon, stars, earth, sea, in an uproar and everyone all over the world in a panic, the wind knocked out of them by the threat of doom, the powers-that-be quaking.

27-28 "And then—then! —they'll see the Son of Man welcomed in grand style—a glorious welcome! When all this starts to happen, up on your feet. Stand tall with your heads high. Help is on the way!"

29-33 He told them a story. "Look at a fig tree. Any tree for that matter. When the leaves begin to show, one look tells you that summer is right around the corner. The same here—when you see these things happen, you know God's kingdom is about here. Don't brush this off: I'm not just saying this for some future generation, but for this one, too—these things will happen. Sky and earth will wear out; my words won't wear out.

34-36 "But be on your guard. Don't let the sharp edge of your expectation get dulled by parties and drinking and shopping. Otherwise, that Day is going to take you by complete surprise, spring on you suddenly like a trap, for it's going to come on everyone, everywhere, at once. So, whatever you do, don't go to sleep at the switch. Pray constantly that you will have the strength and wits to make it through everything that's coming and end up on your feet before the Son of Man."

This is what Advent is really about --- meeting Jesus face to face and that is all that matters.

If you are conflicted by this time of year, you are not alone. But ignore the hoopla and the hype. Don't stress out over things that really don't matter. Take a deep breath, relax and remember what Advent is all about. It is not about shopping. It is about salvation and Christ's return.

A little Advent devotional book, "Proclaiming the Good News of God's Peace [4]", that I have says it well. *"Jesus' teaching was plain and simple --- pay attention. Do not be weighed down and preoccupied with addictions and anxieties. Don't set yourself up to be trapped by your own misguided expectations. Okay, it sounds simple, but in the face of a daily barrage of media hype and advertising, it is a tough order to stay focused and attend to what is truly important.*

"Particularly at this time of year it is all too easy to get caught up in the demands of the holidays. Buy this. Do that. Now more than ever, it is important to listen to the One whose birth [and return] *we celebrate, as he said, 'Be on guard so that your hearts are not weighed down.'"*

Amen.

1. William H. Peterson in <u>Call to Worship</u>, Vol. 46.4, "Advent", Presbyterian Church (U. S. A.), Louisville, KY, 2013
2. Adam Fischer, "Simple Gifts", 201 Advent Calendar in <u>Presbyterians Today</u>, Presbyterian Church (U. S. A.), Louisville, KY, 2012
3. Eugene H. Peterson, <u>The Message</u>: Numbered Edition, NavPress, Colorado Springs, CO, 2005. (Scripture taken from THE MESSAGE. Copyright © 1993, 1994, 1995, 1996, 2000, 2001, 2002. Used by permission of NavPress Publishing Group.)
4. "Proclaiming the Good News, *Advent Devotions 2006*, Presbyterian Church (USA), Louisville, KY, 2006.

You Can't Buy God's Grace
(A Sermon for Epiphany or Baptism of the Lord Sunday)
Luke 3:15-17, 21-22
Acts 8:14-23

I had a wealth of scripture to choose from this morning. Baptism of the Lord Sunday and Epiphany, the 12th Day of Christmas, are only a few days apart. At Epiphany we celebrate the coming of the Magi and their presentation of gifts of gold, frankincense and myrrh to the infant Jesus. The Magi came to worship the Christ Child and brought very valuable gifts. The story is the climax to the Christmas season and we pastors have four suggested scripture readings from which to choose.

For the Baptism of our Lord we have four additional scripture selections. Obviously eight scripture readings in a bit much. I have opted to use the Lectionary suggested Psalm for Baptism of the Lord along with the suggested readings from Luke 3 and Acts 8, but I did make one change. The reading from Acts is suggested as verses 14 through 17 which omits Peter and John laying their hands on the Samaritans so that they receive the Holy Spirit. I added verses 18-23 about Simon the magician because these verses tell an important story we often don't hear in church --- a story of an effort to buy God's grace.

First let's consider the reading from Luke 3 which tells of John the Baptizer baptizing for the repentance of sins. He tells of the Messiah, Jesus, who will baptize with the Holy Spirit and fire. John says that he is not worthy to untie the thongs of Jesus' sandals. To understand the meaning of this comment, consider that in Biblical times a disciple was expected to do almost any kind of menial task for his master, even those things that a slave would do, save one --- the untying of the master's sandals. Disciples were exempted from this task because it was considered to be too degrading yet John states that he is unworthy to carry out even this lowly duty.

John also says, referring to Jesus, that *"He will baptize you with the Holy Spirit. His winnowing fork is in his hand to clear his threshing floor and to gather the wheat into his barn, but he will burn up the chaff with unquenchable fire."* (NIV).

When harvesting, wheat was thrown into the air with a

wooden fork, shaped much like today's metal pitchforks. The grain, which was heavy, fell back and the wind would blow the chaff away. The symbolism is that the good people would be separated from the bad, the good receiving the Holy Spirit and the bad receiving eternal judgment.

The Messiah would separate the human wheat from the chaff --- would decide who was worthy to untie his sandals. You couldn't buy your way into acceptance, into salvation, into grace. That depended on how you lived your life.

When Jesus was baptized by John, the Holy Spirit descended upon him like a dove and God said, *"You are my Son, whom I love; with you I am well pleased."* (NIV).

The baptism of Christ symbolized the coming of the Holy Spirit for the first time with baptism, but certainly not the last.

Throughout scripture, whenever people were baptized in Christ's name, the Holy Spirit descended upon them. Often they began to speak in tongues, which is to speak in other languages, as happened at Pentecost. But in today's reading from Acts 8 that didn't happen. The gospel was spreading beyond Israel and the Jews into Samaria and the gentiles but where was the Holy Spirit?

In Acts 1:8, Jesus said to the apostles, *"You will be my witnesses in Jerusalem, and in all Judea and Samaria, and to the ends of the earth."* (NIV). Phillip went to Samaria proclaiming the Messiah, healing the sick, exorcising demons, and baptizing gentiles in the name of Christ but for some reason, the Holy Spirit did not descend initially on those whom he baptized. Peter and John went to Samaria and prayed that the new believers might receive the Holy Spirit laying hands on them. Then they received the Holy Spirit.

Philip, Peter and John had been watched by a local magician named Simon. In the world at that time, magicians were thought to possess secret powers which could help them determine the future of others. Unlike those of us who pay to see Penn and Teller perform their magic tricks on stage, the people believed that these magicians in the Hellenistic world could actually control their lives and they paid the magicians for their services.

Now here we have Philip baptizing and curing people and Peter and John laying on hands and bringing the Holy Spirit to those who had been baptized. This did not bode well for Simon's business. Not at all.

Simon was very popular. The people of Samaria said of

him, *"This man is rightly called the Great Power of God."* (NIV). People paid Simon for his services and he boasted that he was someone great.

Nevertheless, Simon had been baptized but did he truly accept Christ? Apparently not. He followed Philip everywhere and was astonished at what he saw. But he was observing competition that was reducing his influence on the people and hurting his income. It was a catch-22 for Simon. He had claimed to have accepted Christ but that acceptance did not bring what he expected.

Then Peter and John appeared and Simon watched them place their hands on the new believers and those believers received the Pentecost experience --- they received the Holy Spirit. "Ah," said Simon, "I see. To receive spiritual power, all that is needed is to be touched by Peter and John."

Penn and Teller have a weekly TV show in which various magicians perform magic tricks. The show is called, "Fool Us." The magicians are hoping to fool Penn and Teller as to how they did the tricks. It is rare that they are fooled but Simon was fooled by Peter and John. He thought that they were performing a magic trick and he offered to pay them to teach him how they did it. He thought that he could buy their spiritual power just as he could buy virtually anything else that he desired.

He quickly found out that one cannot buy God's grace. You can't buy salvation.

Peter told him, *"Repent of this wickedness and praise the Lord in the hope that he may forgive you for having such a thought in your heart. For I see that you are full of bitterness and captive to sin."*

"May your money perish with you, because you thought you could buy the gift of God with money." (NIV).

You can't buy God's gift of grace and salvation. Jesus did that for you, freely and willingly on the cross. All you need to do is to thankfully accept that gift. It is priceless.

Amen.

Returning to the Mountain
(A Sermon for Transfiguration of the Lord Sunday)
2 Kings 2:1-12; 2 Corinthians 4:3-6; Mark 9:2-9

Some time ago Rev. Jennifer Barchi, pastor at the Dickey Memorial Presbyterian Church in Baltimore, MD published an article on the Internet, "God wasn't waiting for me." When I read it, it got me thinking about the transfiguration of our Lord.

In her article she talked about Peter, James and John, the three apostles who went to the mountaintop with Jesus and saw him transfigured, bathed in holy light, and talking with Moses and Elijah. She commented about the divine power on that mountaintop which brought the three disciples to their knees and wondered if they thought during the two days after Christ's crucifixion, and before his resurrection, about returning to the mountaintop, in her words, *"... hoping to encounter their Lord in dazzling white clothes of heaven as they had before; hoping that though he was dead, he wasn't really gone."*

What Peter, James and John had encountered on that first trip up the mountain with Jesus was God; it was a spiritual encounter, one which they would never forget, and one which I am sure they would have liked to experience again.

Our scripture reading from Mark concludes with the words, *"Jesus gave them orders not to tell anyone what they had seen until the Son of Man had risen from the dead."* (NIV). We can speculate as to why Jesus told them this. I know that had I been on that mountaintop and witnessed what happened there, I would have wanted to tell the whole world about it. But Jesus told the disciples not to talk about it until after his death. Could they have thought that on that mountain they would find the resurrected Christ in all of his glory? Could they once again be able to experience that incredible spiritual encounter again?

What about you? Think back to those things which have happened in your life which have had deep spiritual meaning to you. Have you ever thought about returning to the places where they happened? Have you ever wondered if God would be waiting for you if you returned to those places?

My personal moments of deep spiritual meaning have more often than not occurred on a mountaintop or out in the woods where I could relax and bathe in the glory of God's creation away from the hustle and bustle of town. I experience that often when Betsy and I are camping on the Blue Ridge Parkway and enjoying the magnificent vistas from that incredible road. One of our favorite locations, which unfortunately is now closed to public access because of lack of US Park Service funds, is the small Otter Creek Campground on the Parkway near the James River in Virginia. I can't go back there now and reclaim the spiritual experience of being there, but I often think about it and wonder if God is waiting there for me.

Are there places like that for you? Places you long to return to? Places where you can hopefully relive that earlier spiritual experience?

Many years ago I was attending a church service out in the woods at a Scout camp, Camp Mountaineer near Morgantown, West Virginia, and I had a mountaintop spiritual experience with the message that the leader of the service shared that day. He read a story that was meant for young boys but which deeply affected me. I have read that story many times since then and on several occasions have used it as a sermon. Each time it nearly brings tears to my eyes as it brings back that first spiritual experience to me. The story is "Gorm, the Giant of the Club," [1] by Ernest Thompson Seaton, one of the founders of Scouting in the United States.

Our three scripture readings all deal with deep spiritual experiences. The reading from 2nd Kings about Elijah and Elisha speaks of God's awesome power as Elijah ascends in a whirlwind to heaven.

Paul's words in 2nd Corinthians speak of light shining out of the darkness to give us the light of knowing the glory of God in the face of Christ Jesus.

Mark describes the transfiguration of our Lord, his conversing with ghosts, Moses and Elijah, and the voice of God saying, *"This is my Son, whom I love. Listen to him!"* (NIV).

These were all incredible spiritual experiences. Wouldn't you want to experience them again if you had been there?

In 2nd Corinthians, Paul says, *"For what we preach is not ourselves, but Jesus Christ as Lord, and ourselves as your servants for Jesus' sake. For God, who said, 'Let light shine out of darkness,' made his light shine in our hearts to give us the light of the knowledge of God's glory displayed in the face of Christ."* (NIV).

Think about that. Your faith, your prayers, your worship and your speaking about Christ is reliving your spiritual experience. That is true of all of us. It may not seem like we are returning to the mountaintop, but we are.

Rev. Jack Haberer, the former editor of <u>Presbyterian Outlook</u> said, *"Did the transfiguration solve the mysteries of the ages, or did it raise more questions in the minds of the apostles? ... First and most obviously it revealed that Jesus is above and beyond anything they had yet conceived. Of major importance was his elevation in significance by the father of the law, Moses, and by the father of the prophets, Elijah. In the process, all the teachings about God communicated in the Hebrew scriptures are now finding their embodiment in the message, the mission, and the person of Jesus."* (2)

We are transfigured many times in many ways. We have many deep spiritual experiences and often don't realize it. Our spiritual experiences happen every day --- seeing the face of a father taking his child to the park, an elderly neighbor cutting flowers in her garden, hearing a symphony orchestra playing a concert, and much more. Have you ever walked on a beach listening to the waves coming ashore or watched your grandchild playing in a pile of leaves? There are thousands of ways in which we are touched by God, ways in which we are almost unbelievingly transfigured. For me it happens when I sit high up on a mountain and look out over the beauty of God's creation which surrounds me. The transfiguration of Jesus, in a way, is also my transfiguration.

But we don't have to think about returning to the mountaintop as the three apostles might have and as I like to do.

We just need to think about our faith, our spiritual experiences, and the wonders of God's creation in our lives --- the smile on the face of our child or grandchild, the beauty of the foliage in the fall, the flowers of the spring, and the majesty of God's creation everywhere.

Do that and you will be transfigured again and again.

Alleluia! Amen!

---

1. *Gorm, the Giant of the Club*, in Julia M. Seaton, <u>Trail & Camp-fire Stories</u>, Seaton Village Press, Santa Fe, NM, 1968 (out of print but copies may be available on the used book market).
2. Jack Haberer, <u>God Views</u>. Geneva Press, Louisville, KY 2001.

Living on Grace Street
(A Sermon for Lent)
1 Peter 3:18-22

This message comes from an unusual direction. I chose the title of this sermon long before I read the scripture for this, the first Sunday of Lent, and before I had any idea of what I was going to say. The title came to me when my wife Betsy and I were driving home from a trip to Florida. Passing through Ft. Myers, Florida I saw a sign, Grace Street, and it struck me that that was what being a Christian means --- we are all living on Grace Street.

Most of you have probably lived in the same place for a long time and very likely have only had two or three addresses at most. I tried to count the many places that I have lived and can remember fourteen streets in five different states. I am sure that there are more addresses that I have forgotten. My life has taken me to many places --- Laclede Street, Shiloh Avenue, Forbes Avenue, Ross Street, Lebanon Avenue, several numbered streets, and many others --- sometimes for just a few months and sometimes for many years. My home has been on many streets but one thing I know is that I am living on Grace Street and have lived there all of my life.

Does that sound strange? It shouldn't. You too live on Grace Street, not US 221, Lake Tahoma Road, Lukin Street or Plantation Drive. Those are the locations of your homes but you really live on Grace Street. You live in the grace of our Lord and Savior Jesus Christ.

Lent and the coming of Easter define what Christianity is all about --- salvation, that is grace, grace given to us when we were baptized. That is what our scripture reading from 1st Peter is telling us.

Let me read it again, this time from Eugene Peterson's Bible paraphrase, <u>The Message</u> [1]:

"That's what Christ did definitively: suffered because of others' sins, the Righteous One for the unrighteous ones. He went through it all—was put to death and then made alive—to bring us to God.

"He went and proclaimed God's salvation to earlier generations who ended up in the prison of judgment because they wouldn't listen. You know, even though God waited patiently all the days that Noah built his ship, only a

few were saved then, eight to be exact—saved from the water by the water. The waters of baptism do that for you, not by washing away dirt from your skin but by presenting you through Jesus' resurrection before God with a clear conscience. Jesus has the last word on everything and everyone, from angels to armies. He's standing right alongside God, and what he says goes."

When you accepted Jesus as your Lord and Savior when you were baptized, or when your parents did it on your behalf as an infant, you moved to Grace Street.

M. Craig Barnes [2] said the *"Grace means that we receive what we need, not what we deserve."*

In Christian theology we call this concept, "justification by grace." In his book <u>Christian Doctrine</u> [3], Shirley Guthrie explains justification by grace with these words: *"The doctrine of justification is a call first of all to give up. Surrender. Stop trying to be something you are not ... You cannot justify yourself. Only God can make things right within you and in your personal relationships ... Justification by grace, as a 'gift,' means quite simply: You do not have to try to buy God's love and acceptance, because you are <u>already</u> loved and accepted by God --- without any qualification of prerequisites ... God says simply, 'I love you just as you are --- <u>you</u>, not your righteousness, your humility, your faith or your accomplishments of one kind or another.'"*

That is what living on Grace Street means.

Some time ago, the Rev. Billy Graham was asked the question, *"Is there any way I can know --- really know --- that I am going to heaven when I die? I believe in Jesus and have given my life to him, but I still can't say that I know beyond doubt."*

Billy Graham replied, *"Imagine that you owed the bank an enormous amount of money --- far beyond your ability to repay, even in the best of times. Even if you worked hard for the rest of your life, you knew you'd never be able to earn enough to pay this debt and yet it had to be repaid or you'd lose everything.*

"But suppose the banker's son came along and befriended you --- and not only that, he offered to pay the debt for you.

"This is somewhat similar to what Jesus Christ did for you. You owed God a debt --- caused by sin. And you could never be good enough to erase that debt. But Jesus Christ did it for you. He paid the price, and now our sins are forgiven --- completely!

"Christ has made you a member of his family forever --- and nothing can ever change that. His love for you will never end and will carry you to eternal life in heaven."

I add that Christ is your good neighbor on Grace Street. Like a good neighbor, Jesus is there.

Some years ago a friend in Nova Scotia sent me an email with a story of God's grace. That email said:

There once was a man named George Thomas, pastor in a small New England town. One Easter Sunday morning he came to the Church carrying a rusty, bent, old bird cage, and set it by the pulpit. Eyebrows were raised and, as if in response, Pastor Thomas began to speak.

"I was walking through town yesterday when I saw a young boy coming toward me swinging this bird cage. On the bottom of the cage were three little wild birds, shivering with cold and fright. I stopped the lad and asked, "What do you have there, son?"

"Just some old birds," came the reply.

"What are you going to do with them?" I asked.

"Take 'em home and have fun with 'em," he answered. "I'm gonna' tease 'em and pull out their feathers to make 'em fight. I'm gonna' have a really good time."

"But you'll get tired of those birds sooner or later. What will you do then?"

"Oh, I got some cats," said the little boy. "They like birds. I'll take 'em to them."

The pastor was silent for a moment. "How much do you want for those birds, son?"

"Huh? Why, you don't want them birds, mister. They're just plain old field birds. They don't sing. They ain't even pretty!"

"How much?" the pastor asked again.

The boy sized up the pastor as if he were crazy and said, "$10?"

The pastor reached in his pocket and took out a ten-dollar bill. He placed it in the boy's hand. In a flash, the boy was gone. The pastor picked up the cage and gently carried it to the end of the alley where there was a tree and a grassy spot. Setting the cage down, he opened the door, and by softly tapping the bars persuaded the birds out, setting them free.

Well, that explained the empty bird cage on the pulpit, and then the pastor began to tell this story:

One day Satan and Jesus were having a conversation. Satan had just come from the Garden of Eden, and he was gloating and boasting. "Yes, sir, I just caught a world full of people down there. Set me a trap, used bait I knew they couldn't resist. Got 'em all!"

"What are you going to do with them?" Jesus asked.

Satan replied, "Oh, I'm gonna' have fun! I'm gonna' teach them how to marry and divorce each other, how to hate and abuse each other, how to drink and smoke and curse. I'm gonna' teach them how to invent guns and bombs and kill each other. I'm really gonna' have fun!"

"And what will you do when you are done with them?" Jesus asked.

"Oh, I'll kill 'em," Satan glared proudly.

"How much do you want for them?" Jesus asked.

"Oh, you don't want those people. They ain't no good. Why, you'll take them and they'll just hate you? They'll spit on you, curse you and kill you. You don't want those people!"

"How much? He asked again.

Satan looked at Jesus and sneered, "All your blood, tears and your life."

Jesus said, "DONE!" Then He paid the price.

The pastor picked up the cage and walked from the pulpit.

Amen.

1. Eugene H. Peterson, The Message: Numbered Edition, NavPress, Colorado Springs, CO, 2005. (Scripture taken from THE MESSAGE. Copyright © 1993, 1994, 1995, 1996, 2000, 2001, 2002. Used by permission of NavPress Publishing Group.)
2. M. Craig Barnes, The Pastor as a Minor Poet, William B. Eerdsmans Publishing Co., Grand Rapids, MI 2009.
3. Shirley Guthrie, Christian Doctrine, Westminster John Knox Press, Louisville, 1994

Justification by Grace
(A Sermon for Easter Sunday)
Acts 10:34-43
1 Corinthians 15:1-11

Typically on Easter Sunday, you hear a sermon on a Bible passage from one of the four Gospels. The four passages are the first verses of Matthew 28, Mark 16, Luke 24 and John 20. Each tells the story of the women going to the tomb and finding it empty. Depending on which gospel you read, how they react to the empty tomb varies but the message is the same, **Christ has risen**. For this message I have chosen passages from Acts and 1st Corinthians instead of one of the more traditional gospel passages. We know the gospel stories quite well but do we really understand what the resurrection of Christ truly meant? I am sure that the women at the tomb and the apostles at that point in time really did not understand, but they certainly came to understand. Today I want to tell you the meaning of the resurrection and what it means to all of us personally, not to restate the resurrection story that we all know so well. Hence my choice of a passage from Acts and an Epistle reading from 1st Corinthians.

If you have ever been to a Presbytery meeting, you will know that any time a minister joins the Presbytery or when a pastor is commissioned to a church, that person is asked a question to be answered publically before Presbytery. The question is chosen from a list of standard questions. The purpose of the public answer is to give the ministers and elders at the meeting a glimpse of the viewpoints of the individual who has been called to a church or who is new to the Presbytery.

A pastor might be asked something like, "How would you explain the authority of scripture to a class for new members?" or "How would you explain to an elder what happens at the baptismal font and at the communion table?" These are questions which obviously have deep theological significance.

Questions might lean more to other functions of a pastor such as asking, "When a person comes to you with a serious ethical problem, what theological resources do you use in advising that person?"

They might be more of an administrative nature such as, "What would you like to change about the *Book of Order*?" Considering how complex the Presbyterian *Book of Order* is, I might get tempted, if asked that question, to give a one-word facetious answer – "Everything!"

Joking aside, as you can see, the questions a pastor might be asked are very wide ranging and can touch on any or all aspects of ministry – theology, scripture, administrative matters, counseling, and so forth.

Pastors are not caught by surprise with the choice of questions --- not at all. They are always told in advance what question they will be asked. It is not a test or a "pop quiz." That is not its purpose at all. Rather it is a way of introducing the pastor to Presbytery and also to the church which he or she will be serving.

I have gone through this process more than once. The first time was when I was called as co-pastor of the First Presbyterian Church in Bessemer City, NC. The question I was asked at that time was, in my judgment, the least meaningful of a long list of questions, any one of which would have been better. I was asked, "What resources have you found most helpful as a pastor?"

Now that is a pretty bland question and can be readily answered rather simplistically. I listed a number of things which are rather obvious --- prayer, scripture, the confessions of the church, the people of the congregation, books and even the Internet. That was all well and good but it certainly did not give me the chance to really express my beliefs or my approach to ministry. I thought to myself, "Of all of the things they could have asked me, surely they could have asked a question which is more meaningful than this!"

Well, they didn't. They ask only one question and the pastor has about a minute to answer, so that was it.

The second time I wondered if I would be asked such a question again or if I would be given a more deeply theological one.

After I met with the Committee on Ministry and was approved by them to accept the call to Conley Memorial Presbyterian Church in Marion, NC, I waited several weeks wondering what I might be asked. Then I received an email from Presbytery with the question. As it turns out, it wasn't a question at all. I was asked to make a statement to describe a theological theme or doctrine that is fruitful in my ministry. Wow! What a change from the last time! This time I had been given the chance to truly express my deep felt theological beliefs.

I realized immediately that I could, in truth, answer rather simply with only three words --- three words which are the substance of the meaning of Easter --- three words which are directly reflected in our two scripture readings today. Those words are "justification by grace." Of course, I didn't respond simply with three words --- although at one Presbytery meeting I attended some time ago one minister actually gave a one-word answer to a question and it was acceptable. The number of words used is not important – the meaning of the answer is. I gave a longer answer but, in substance, my answer was those three words, my sermon title, "Justification by grace."

Now what do those three words mean? One problem with pastors and theologians, and for that matter with any profession, is "shop talk." We use words in talking to others which are not necessarily understood by others outside of our profession. We do that and sometimes forget to explain ourselves – so please let me explain.

What is "justification"? What does it mean in theological terms?

Justification, according to the *Holman Illustrated Bible Dictionary* [1] is *"Divine, forensic act of God, based on the work of Christ upon the cross, whereby a sinner is pronounced righteous by the imputation of the righteousness of Christ."*

That definition has some two dollar words in it and boiling it down to simpler terms it simply states the most fundamental belief of Christianity --- that is that our sins are indeed forgiven through the act of God in the sacrifice of Christ on the cross.

The other word, "grace" is defined as, *"Undeserved acceptance and love received from another."* In the Biblical context, *"It refers to the undeserved favor of God in providing salvation for those deserving condemnation"* --- that is all sinners --- all of us.

Those three words, "justification by grace", taken together simply mean that through God's love for us, Christ died on the cross as a sacrifice to insure forgiveness of our sins and to provide salvation to us, even though we don't deserve it.

That is pretty powerful and is the gist of what Christianity is all about --- what Easter is all about!

In his commentary on the book of Acts, William Barclay [2] refers to our reading from Acts as "The Heart of the Gospel", and so it is. In the reading Luke is reporting on Peter's description of the essence of his preaching. Barclay summarizes the essence of Peter's preaching with six points:

1. The coming of Jesus was due to the true love of God.
2. Jesus' ministry was one of healing and of his great desire to rid the world of sorrow and pain.
3. The crucifixion was a huge example of what human sin can do. Jesus who was truly without sin was condemned through an incredibly sinful act of humans.
4. Jesus could not be defeated. He conquered the worst humans could do. He conquered death.
5. Peter was a witness. He didn't hear about Jesus. He knew him and was witness to the resurrection. Jesus was a living presence.
6. The result is forgiveness of sins and a new relationship with God. The friendship which should always have existed between humankind and God had been interrupted by sin but, through Jesus that friendship has dawned upon humankind.

In 1st Corinthians, Paul recapitulates this. He tells about God's gift in Christ and explains that all of humankind is justified by grace, Jesus having been given as the ultimate sacrifice. Paul persecuted Christians, he stood by and encouraged the stoning of Stephen, Jesus appeared to him on the road to Damascus, and he became Christ's greatest apostle. He received Christ's justification and God's grace.

So, how exactly did I answer that question at the Presbytery meeting? Yes, I could have simply said say, "Justification by grace" and I am sure that would have been OK, after all I would be using "shop talk" and the clergy present would understand it fully. But I did not do that. What I told them is that some years ago a pastor said to me that he really preached most of the time on only one of two things. When he said that, I did not understand what he meant. His sermons were wide ranging and I could not see how he felt that he was preaching on only two subjects. But now, having served as a pastor and having preached in many churches, I know exactly what he meant. He was referring to two primary theological doctrines and the same is true for me. What I do and what I say from the pulpit are founded on the everlasting love of God and on justification by grace brought to us through Christ's crucifixion and our acceptance of him as Lord and Savior, in other words, the story of what Easter truly means.

That is the Easter message, a message which applies 52 weeks a year, not just on Easter Sunday.
Amen!

1. <u>Holman Illustrated Bible Dictionary</u>, Holman Bible Publishers, Nashville, 2003
2. William Barclay, <u>The Acts of the Apostles</u>, rev. ed., Westminster Press, Philadelphia, 1976

A Divine Gift
(A Sermon for Pentecost)
John 14:8-17, 25-27

One of my Bible commentaries comments that preaching on anything from John 14 to 17 is easier said than done, saying that its phrases invite the hearer to boredom.

In the original Greek these parts of John's Gospel are said to be tolerable but in translation to English, not so much so.

John Calvin's solution to the problem was to say that every literate Christian should be taught Greek. That would presumably solve the problem but obviously is rather impractical so I instead will try in this message to make sense out of portions of John 14 in English and hopefully keep them from being boring to you.

Our scripture reading is about a divine gift given to all of us. That gift, in Greek, is parakletos. In English it is often written as Paraclete, a word which really doesn't have a clear translation into English. Some Bible translations use the word *"Counselor"*. Others use *"Advocate"*. The King James Bible uses the word *"Comforter"* and the Good News Bible uses *"Helper"*. <u>The Message</u>, Eugene Peterson's Bible paraphrase, calls the Paraclete *"Friend"*.

Counselor, Advocate, Comforter, Helper, Friend --- those words all have different meanings to us. *Advocate* tends to suggest a lawyer --- someone who stands up and fights for us in court. A *helper* is one who lends us a hand in whatever we try to do. A *comforter* is available to give us a shoulder to cry on when we are experiencing stress. A *counselor* gives us advice and helps us to sort out whatever is on our mind. A friend is with us in good times and bad. Yes, defining the Paraclete is difficult to do precisely and in our scripture reading Jesus is trying to explain it to the disciples. He is trying to explain a divine gift --- the Holy Spirit --- and he is having trouble making them understand. Can you define the Holy Spirit precisely? I don't think so.

We talk about the three parts of the Godhead, another difficult word to define --- the Father, the Son, and the Holy Spirit – one God in three parts – the Trinity. Try to explain that. It is difficult.

That was Philip's problem in our scripture reading. He asks Jesus to show the Father to the disciples. He wants to see God with his own eyes. If he can see, he will believe. He will be satisfied.

Jesus responds that whoever has seen him has seen the Father. *"Seeing, believing, and knowing God are all based on the concrete, physical works that Jesus has done in Philip's presence."* [1]

Jesus says, *"If you cannot believe that I am with God as a metaphysical proposition, you can at least believe me for who I am, because the remarkable things I do show that I am in the Father and the Father is in me ...' The kind of knowing of which Jesus speaks springs from seeing with the eyes of faith."* (ibid).

Jesus tells the disciples that he is going to the Father but that the Paraclete, the divine gift, is coming to be with them until he returns. The divine gift is the Holy Spirit which will reside with them, which will teach them, which will dwell within them, and which will be a living link to Jesus. He says that the world will no longer see him but the disciples will see him. The third part of the Trinity, the Holy Spirit, the divine gift, will remain with them and be present and among all believers.

The Spirit came upon Jesus at his baptism and Jesus baptized with the Holy Spirit. Now he is promising his followers that when he ascends to heaven, they will receive the divine gift of the Holy Spirit. His ascension is the precondition for them to receive this divine gift. They are promised that when they do receive this gift, they will be enabled to continue the work of Jesus and to do even greater works; they will be heard and their prayers will be answered to meet the needs of what they have to do; and they will be accompanied in their life and mission in the world by the Spirit. Unlike Jesus who is departing, the Spirit will be with them forever. [2]

This promise of Christ came to pass at Pentecost, 50 days after his resurrection and ten days after his ascension. The Holy Spirit descended with noise and tongues of fire and people began to speak in other languages. The Holy Spirit remains with us today. Unfortunately, very few of us today can speak in other languages but some can and I envy them. I can speak bits and pieces of a number of languages, just enough to make a fool of myself unlike a friend in the Netherlands who could speak at least 12 languages fluently. Speaking in tongues was a necessity for the apostles but is not for us, at least not many of us.

However, the promise which Jesus made to the disciples was a promise to us as well. We and believers everywhere are also recipients of the divine gift of the Holy Spirit. **Alleluia. Amen.**

1. Lamar Williamson, Jr., <u>Preaching John</u>, Westminster John Knox Press, Louisville, 2004.
2. Fred B. Craddock, et al, <u>Preaching Through the Christian Year</u>, Year C, Trinity Press International, Valley Forge, PA, 1994.

Three Gods or One?
(A Sermon for Trinity Sunday)
Isaiah 6:1-8; John 3:1-17

Some years ago I was teaching a class in Riyadh, the capital of Saudi Arabia. My host was an Arab, a Muslim. The form of Islam practiced in Saudi Arabia is known as Wahhabism, an ultra-conservative form of Sunni Islam.

My host was very interested in the fact that I am a Presbyterian and, using a common misunderstanding in the Muslim world, said that Christianity was wrong because Christians worship three gods, not one. He conceded that Christians do worship the God of Abraham, as do Muslims and Jews. That was OK to him but the problem in his eyes was those other two gods, Jesus and the Holy Spirit.

Clearly he had absolutely no conception at all of a Trinitarian God. I tried to explain the Trinity to him but I got nowhere. He was convinced that I was a misguided infidel, and he gave me several religious tracts, which incidentally were published by the Saudi military, which argued against the idea of the Trinity. He wanted me to "see the light" and was trying hard to convert me to the Islamic way of thinking. Before I left Saudi Arabia he gave me an English language copy of the Quran, the Muslim holy book.

In Islam Jesus is recognized as one of the major holy prophets --- Adam, Noah, Abraham, Moses, Mohammed and Jesus. Of these they believe that only one, Jesus of Nazareth, was without sin, but in their eyes Jesus was a human, a very good human, but a human none the less. Certainly he could not have been a god.

Almost anything you write or say in Saudi Arabia is ended with the words "Insha'Allah," meaning "If God is willing".

"Have a good day, Insha'Allah"

"I pray that my son is cured of his medical problem, Insha'Allah"

"I pray for peace in the world, Insha'Allah"

"Insha'Allah" is almost like a period at the end of sentences. The most minor thing or a prayer for a miracle always ends, "Insha'Allah."

What, in my mind my host was really doing when he said

"Insha'Allah," was calling upon the Holy Spirit. He was invoking the presence of God all around him, but he just couldn't recognize that.

In Saudi Arabia, no vestige of any religion other than Islam is permitted. A Christian entering the country with a Bible will have it taken away. I even saw a customs agent tear up an ordinary calendar that a passenger on my plane had in his suitcase. The calendar we use has the Christian era as its basis. Thus it is not tolerated in Saudi Arabia. I could go on to point out other Wahhabi religious customs but that is not my purpose today.

Today is Trinity Sunday, the day each year that we hear sermons about the Trinity, what it is and what it isn't. The concept of the Trinity is almost as confusing to many Christians as it is to the Islamic world.

How can we say that we worship one God, the God of Abraham, Isaac and Jacob, in one breath and then talk about a Godhead --- Father, Son and Holy Spirit? It is a tough concept. It is no wonder that my host in Saudi Arabia didn't understand it. Many Christians don't understand it either.

Charles Wiley put the concept well in an article for *Presbyterians Today*. His article was entitled "Reclaiming the Trinity." [1] The "punch line" of the article said, *"The Trinity is not an optional 'extra' to God; it is the very nature of God as revealed to us in scripture."* The Trinity is the very nature of God.

In our scripture reading from Isaiah, the prophet is attempting to describe the nature of God in allegorical terms. The reading from John, perhaps the most well-known passage in the New Testament, tries to describe the nature of God as well. In it, Nicodemus, a Pharisee, is listening to Jesus and is trying to understand him. Nicodemus was a good man, a theologian, who had the very traditional outlook of the Pharisees, an outlook which was just as rigid as was that of my host in Saudi Arabia. Jesus is telling him that to enter the kingdom of God, one must be born of water and Spirit --- water alluding to baptism and the Spirit being the Holy Spirit. Nicodemus didn't understand and Jesus asked, *"You are Israel's teacher and you do not understand these things?"* (NIV).

The Jewish law, the Torah, and the later prophetic books of the Old Testament were what the Pharisees studied. They were the Hebrew Scriptures and were the basis of Jewish beliefs. Nowhere in those laws was there any such concept as the Trinity. Nicodemus had the same mental block as that of my host in Saudi Arabia.

Certainly the prophets talked about the coming of a

Messiah, but to them the Messiah was a human, not God. Nicodemus was witness to many things which Jesus did but he certainly didn't, at least at that point in time, believe that Jesus was the Son of God; a great man, yes! The Messiah, possibly! But not God.

Any time an ordination takes place in the Presbyterian Church, an ordination of ruling elders, ministers, deacons and Commissioned Pastors, the question is always asked: *"Do you trust in Jesus Christ your Savior, acknowledge him Lord of all and Head of the Church, and through him believe in one God, Father, Son, and Holy Spirit?"*

I have never heard anyone say "No!" in answer to that question. Have you? That's not very likely.

But Charles Wiley argues that many Presbyterians answer that question in the affirmative, and then tend to become functional Unitarians. We talk about our faith through simple appeals to God: "God loves you, God forgives you, God will be with you," and so on. We simplify things and take the easy way out. We don't try to explain the Trinity --- we ignore it --- because we often don't understand it even though we sing, "God in three persons, blessed Trinity."

Quoting Charles Wiley, *"The language of Father, Son and Holy Spirit, etched in scripture and creed, remains indispensable for our efforts to speak faithfully of God. This is especially true regarding baptism in the name of the Triune God, one of the few things that connect Christian believers around the world...*

"Creator/Redeemer/Sustainer is a wonderful description of the work of God on our behalf. It is Trinitarian in the sense that each person of the Trinity is involved in the functions of creating, redeeming and sustaining us. But it cannot be understood that one person of the Trinity is creator, a second redeemer and the third sustainer." All three persons are the creator, the redeemer and the sustainer.

When I was thinking about this sermon, I mentioned it to our daughter Karen, and said how hard it is to explain the Trinity. She said, "Do you remember the book I gave you, <u>The Shack</u>. That explains the Trinity better than anything I have ever seen." I had forgotten about that book, but Karen was right.

The author of <u>The Shack</u> is a Canadian, William P. Young. The main character, Mack, takes three of his five children on a camping trip. Two of the children are canoeing when the canoe overturns, one child almost drowns and Mack rushes into the water to save him leaving his young daughter Missy alone.

The boy is saved but when they return to the campsite, Missy is missing. Police are called and it is soon discovered that Missy had been abducted and murdered by a serial killer. Her bloody clothing is found at an abandoned shack in the woods but her body is never found. Mack sinks into deep depression and remorse.

Then Mack receives a note in his mailbox from someone signed "Papa" asking Mack to meet him at the shack. Mack's wife always referred to God as Papa and Mack wonders if the note is from God.

Mack's family goes to visit relatives and Mack goes back to that shack in the woods for the weekend. There he encounters three manifestations of God, an African American woman who calls herself Papa; a Middle-Eastern carpenter, you know who he is; and an Asian woman named Sarayu, the manifestation of the Holy Spirit.

Mack meets with each of them in turn and has various experiences with them over the three days --- he walks across a lake with the carpenter, Jesus; he sees an image of his father in heaven with Sarayu, the Holy Spirit; he talks to a personification of God's wisdom; and he goes on a hike with Papa, God, and finds Missy's body in a cave.

After the weekend, Mack heads home and is so preoccupied and inattentive at what happened that he is nearly killed in an automobile accident.

After he recovers, he realizes that he really did not spend the weekend at the shack, the accident actually occurred on the day he arrived there. But he is able to lead the police to Missy's body and enough forensic evidence is found at the scene to identify the killer.

Certainly, this is a piece of fiction but it does illustrate how God interacts in our lives. God appears to us in whatever form is most necessary and appropriate at any given point in time --- as the Father --- or as the Son --- or as the Holy Spirit.

That is what the Trinity is all about.

Amen.

1. Charles Wiley, "Reclaiming the Trinity", *Presbyterians Today*, June 2011

It's a Puzzlement
(A Sermon for Trinity Sunday)
Romans 5:1-5; John 16:12-15

You may have seen the movie, "The King and I" starring Yul Brynner and Deborah Kerr. It is a beautiful musical production about a Welch governess who is hired to be the nanny and teacher for the many children of the King of Siam.

The culture clash between this outspoken woman from the British Isles and the absolute monarch of Siam forms the gist of the story. If you have not seen it, look it up on Netflix or Amazon.com. It is a great way to spend a few hours watching a good story and enjoying some fine music.

In one scene of the film, Yul Brynner, the King, gets confused over something Deborah Kerr says and ponders it saying, *"It's a puzzlement."*

Trinity Sunday is the Sunday after Pentecost when the Holy Spirit descended on the apostles and the crowd in Jerusalem for the annual Pentecost festival.

What is the Holy Spirit? What exactly did the descent of the Spirit mean? What was Jesus trying to tell the apostles in our scripture reading from John? What is Paul talking about in our reading from Romans when he says that "... The Holy Spirit ...has been given to us"? It's a puzzlement, a real puzzlement indeed.

Let us put our scripture reading from John in context. It is the night before Jesus was arrested. Jesus had told the apostles that he would be betrayed and that he would be denied. Peter protested and Jesus told Peter that he would deny him three times before the cock crowed at dawn.

The Rev. Shannon Kershner, former pastor of the Black Mountain Presbyterian Church and now head of staff at one of the four largest Presbyterian churches in the country gave a sermon in Montreat, North Carolina at a meeting of the Presbytery of Western North Carolina in which she addressed this "puzzlement" --- what we call the Doctrine of the Trinity.

Rev. Kershner said, *"What on earth could be more difficult to hear, to bear, than the truth that their beloved friend was going to suffer and die; and furthermore, at least one of them, would betray him; and at least one of them, maybe all of them, would deny him?"*

Jesus told them, "I have much more to say to you, more than you can bear." What did he mean? It's a puzzlement.

Then Jesus muddies the water even more saying, *"But when he, the Spirit of truth comes, he will guide you into all the truth."* What is this Spirit? It's a puzzlement.

This Spirit is the third part of what we call the Trinity --- Father, Son and Holy Spirit. But what is the Trinity? It's a puzzlement for most Christians and even for us pastors.

Barbara Brown Taylor [1] commented that the doctrine of the Trinity was *a "logic buster".*

It's a puzzlement.

She said further that the Bible itself compounds the problem because scripture makes it sound as if the three parts of the Trinity are independent of each other. Jesus says that he is going to the Father but that, once he is gone, he will send an Advocate, the Holy Spirit.

It's a puzzlement and it will probably always be a puzzlement.

St. Patrick tried to explain the Trinity with a shamrock which has three co-equal leaves but still is one plant.

Others, including me, have tried to explain it with water. Water can be ice, a solid; a liquid; or steam, a gas --- but it can't be all three at the same time.

According to Shirley C. Guthrie, Jr. [2], *"... the doctrine of the Trinity is ... the church's admittedly inadequate way of trying to understand and guard against false interpretation of the uniquely Biblical-Christian understanding of who God is, what God is like, how and where God is at work in the world, what God thinks about us human beings, does for us, requires of us, promises us.*

"Christians do not believe in the doctrine of the Trinity ... We believe in a living God. But the God we believe in is the God this doctrine confesses, the one living and true God who is Father, Son, and Holy Spirit. Faith in this God --- and lives shaped by faith in this God --- is what distinguishes Christians from people who do not believe in God at all and from other religious people whose faith and life is shaped by other views of God."

It's a puzzlement --- but does it matter?

In God's own good time there will no longer be a puzzlement. He was with us in the beginning as Creator. He came as the Son, our Redeemer. He is now with us as the Holy Spirit, as our Counselor.

As Paul reminds us in our reading from Romans 5, *"Therefore, since we have been justified through faith, we have peace with God through our*

Lord Jesus Christ, through whom we have gained access by faith into this grace in which we now stand. And we boast in the hope of the glory of God. Not only so, but we also glory in our sufferings, because we know that suffering produces perseverance; perseverance, character; and character, hope. And hope does not put us to shame, because God's love has been poured out into our hearts through the Holy Spirit, who has been given to us." (NIV)

Yes, it's a puzzlement. But what a wonderful puzzlement it is.
Amen.

1. Barbara Brown Taylor, Home by Another Way, Cowley Publications, Cambridge, MA, 1999. All rights reserved.
2. Shirley C. Guthrie, Jr., Christian Doctrine, rev. ed., Westminster John Knox Press, Louisville, KY, 1994.

She Gave All That She Had
(A Stewardship Sermon)

Mark 12:38-44

I own four coins that are more than 2000 years old --- coins from the time of Christ. One coin is a denarius of Emperor Tiberius. It dates from 14-37 AD, the time of Christ. It is made of silver and was the most common major coin of that time. A denarius was the daily wage for a soldier or an unskilled worker. Therefore, a denarius was the equivalent of our minimum daily wage, currently about $60 in the United States. You can buy quite a lot of bread for $60.

Two of the coins are prutahs. One is from the reign of Herod the Great in Judah and dates from the period 40-4 BC. The other is from the reign of Herod Archelaus who ruled from 4 BC to 6 AD. Like our modern coins, these coins remained in circulation for many years and were common during the time of Christ. It took 10 prutahs to buy a loaf of bread, so you can see that they did not have a great value in comparison to a denarius.

The fourth coin is a lepton from the reign of Pontius Pilate. It was minted around 31 AD as best we can tell and could well have been touched by Jesus or one of his disciples. The value of the lepton was one-half of a prutah so it took 20 of these small coins to purchase a loaf of bread. The lepton was the lowest value coin in Biblical times. This is the coin known as the "widow's mite," the coin referred to in Mark 12:42. The lepton's value was so small that, like our penny, some people wouldn't even bend over to pick it up if they dropped it. Nevertheless, two leptons were all that the widow had, and she gave those two small coins to the temple.

Widows in the ancient world had a very difficult life. Unless they had sons to care for them, it was extremely difficult for them to survive. It was a paternalistic society and women, particularly widows, were held in little regard.

To the rich people in the temple that day the widow's contribution would have been sneered at. Most of them probably donated a denarius or two, a sum which would have been very large to the widow but really was insignificant to the rich donors. They weren't placing any hardship on themselves. They could well afford it and probably more. Not so for the widow. Those two leptons could have bought her a small piece of bread. They might have been the difference between her having something to eat or of going without.

This is stewardship season for churches --- the time of year when we are asked to reflect on our level of giving and to decide how we will support the church during the coming year. What would stewardship be without thankful givers? What would it be without the widow's mite?

The Rev. Barbara Brown Taylor [1] asked that question in her book "*The Preaching Life.*" She said, *"It would be like Thanksgiving without turkey, Christmas without presents, Easter without eggs. The story of the widow's mite is the all-time great story of Christian giving, the story of a poor woman who gave everything she had to the church. What the rich ... (man) could not do, she did without being asked, only there was no crowd to witness the liquidation of her estate. It was as easy as uncurling her fingers from around two copper coins and letting them fall into the temple treasury, still damp from her hands, where they made such a small sound that only she could hear it.*

"As far as she knew, no one even saw her. But then again, no one ever saw her. She was one of life's minor characters, one of the invisible people who come and go without anyone noticing what they do, or what they have on, or when they leave the room. She was a bit player, one of the extras who ring the stage while the major characters stride around in the middle, dazzling everyone with their costumes and high drama."

Jesus said, *"Watch out for the teachers of the law. They like to walk around in flowing robes and be greeted in marketplaces, and have the most important seats in the synagogues and the places of honor at banquets. They devour widows' houses and for a show make lengthy prayers. Such men will be punished most severely."* (NIV)

Jesus is referring to the scribes, Jerusalem's elite. They were the official interpreters of scripture. They were the clergy of the day but were not paid as pastors today are paid. They got their income from students, the poor box, and the temple treasury. They also had ways of making a lot more. They were important in their own minds and they played on that importance. They *"wrangled invitations to peoples' homes, for instance, where they accepted the best seats, the best cuts of meat, the best cups of the best wine. When they wore out their welcome, no one dared to tell them so, least of all their poorer parishioners who were glad to spend their savings on such esteemed guests. ...The scribes were clearly the people to watch. They were the guardians of the faith, the religious aristocracy, even if they did sponge off those they were meant to serve."* (Barbara Brown Taylor)

But Jesus was not watching the scribes and their parading about in their impressive robes on center stage, if you will. He was watching an insignificant woman, at least one who was insignificant in the eyes of the scribes and the rich people in the temple. She had nothing --- no food and only a pittance in money which she willingly donated. She was invisible. No one saw her except Jesus.

She made a complete sacrifice, so much so that Jesus called his disciples to witness it, saying, *"I tell you the truth, this poor widow has put more into the treasury than all of the others. They gave out of their wealth; but she, out of her poverty, put in everything --- all she had to live on. (NIV)"*

All we know about this widow is that she gave all that she had. She held nothing back. Her two leptons, one tenth of a loaf of bread, were a fortune in the eyes of God.

Christians aren't asked to give all they have to the work of the Lord, rather we are asked to tithe, to give ten percent one way or another to God's work.

That does not necessarily mean to the church alone. It means to the needy, to social service agencies, to all forms of mission. It also means time --- time serving as a community worker, time serving the church, time working as a youth leader, time working for charities and so forth.

Christ asks that we give back ten percent of everything that has been given to us. That is his criterion but is one which sadly most Christians do not meet.

The *Presbyterian Outlook* reported that a national study found that about one-quarter of the respondents said that they tithed --- that they gave at least ten percent of their income to church and charity.

In fact, when actual donations were compared to the respondents' incomes, only 3 percent of them gave away more than 5 percent of their income. The rest somehow thought that they had given much more than they actually did.

Another study reported that, American Christians still give less than 2 percent of their income to charity.

Earlier studies showed that 20 percent of American Christians gave nothing at all while the top 5 percent provide 60 percent of all donations. The higher level givers gave for various reasons:

--- Some because they had been taught by their parents to do so by example and by what their parents said.

--- Some for theological reasons --- "everything belongs to God including one's material possessions".

--- Some felt a duty to tithe.

--- Some gave in response to the needs of the world.

--- Some gave from guilt, feeling that they were supposed to give.

The lower level givers had different reasons:

--- Some gave only as much as they felt they could afford at a particular moment in time. They had "wealth insecurity", that even if they had assets, the money might somehow be diminished in the future.

--- Some gave only what they felt "comfortable" in giving.

--- Some did not understand how much others tended to give and what constituted generosity.

--- Some were confused about how much they actually gave.

--- Some expressed "comfortable guilt." They felt they should give more but did nothing to change their behavior.

If you are a tither, God is smiling upon you.

If you have not reached that level as yet, for whatever reason, think about the coming year and prayerfully consider how you can make a positive step toward becoming a tither. Whatever you do, God will also be smiling at you.

Amen.

---

1. Barbara Brown Taylor, The Preaching Life, Cowley Publications, Cambridge, MA, 1993. All rights reserved.

King for All Eternity
(A Sermon for Christ the King Sunday)
Psalm 132; Revelation 1:4b-8; John 18:33-37

Christ the King Sunday is the last Sunday of the church year, the Sunday in which we celebrate the salvation given to us through the crucifixion and resurrection of our Lord and in his reigning over us for all eternity. His reign of glory is reflected in our Psalm and in our readings from Revelation and John.

The First Temple in Jerusalem was built by Solomon. Zerubbabel built the Second Temple which was subsequently enlarged by Herod. The Temples were built as homes for God and, in the case of Solomon's Temple, as the place to house the Ark of the Covenant.

That Temple was envisioned by David and that is what Psalm 132 is all about, David's plans for the First Temple. David never built that Temple but eventually it was to be built by his son, Solomon. It effectively was meant to be an earthly palace for God, one which would stand forever as God's home and the eventual home of the King of Kings, the Messiah.

The Temple of Solomon of course did not survive, nor did the Second Temple. Scripturally we know that the reign of David began the line which culminated with Jesus' coming as the Messiah, the Son of God, to assume the holy throne.

Throughout his ministry, Jesus kept asking that his disciples and many of those whom he cured not to tell anyone that he was the Messiah, the King of Kings. He never said that he was the Messiah publicly until he was brought to trial before Pontius Pilate. That admission is stated in our scripture reading from John. Pilate asks him, *"Are you the king of the Jews?"* Jesus' answer was very carefully stated. To claim to be king would be construed by the Romans as rebellion. Perhaps that is why Jesus kept discouraging others from saying that he was the Messiah.

In answer to the question, Jesus replied, *"You have said so."* He turns Pilate's question back on him and then starts to question Pilate. The prisoner is questioning the judge. Can you picture that happening today? If anyone tried that in court today, they would be charged with contempt.

Jesus looks at Pilate and asks if Pilate's question was his

own or if someone else put him up to asking it. What Jesus is doing is trying to communicate one-on-one with Pilate, much as he had done with the Samaritan woman at the well. He is, according to Lamar Williamson [1], *"... giving Pilate a chance to encounter the living Word personally, rather than simply as another case to be adjudicated."*

But Pilate ignores Jesus' question and shows his disdain for his subjects by saying, *"I am not a Jew, am I?"*

Pilate assumes however that the Jewish religious leaders must have some reason for handing Jesus over to Roman authority, but he is clearly more interested in what Jesus has done than what his accusers say about Jesus. He asks, "What have you done?"

The answer from Jesus is not what Pilate expects. Jesus says, *"My Kingdom is not of this world."* Jesus is saying that he is King, but not a king in any sense like an earthly king. Pilate says, *"So you are a king?"* and Jesus replies, *"You are right in saying I am a King. In fact, for this reason I was born, and for this I came into the world to testify to the truth. Everyone on this side of truth listens to me."* (NIV). Jesus has now publicly identified himself as the Messiah, the King of Kings. He is the one to assume the throne David hoped to build so many centuries before, but it is a heavenly throne, not anything on earth.

According to Lamar Williamson [1], *"Jesus opens the door of life to Pilate, but Pilate turns his back and walks away. His interest is in Roman law and in maintenance of order and his own authority. Jesus poses no threat to public order, nor has he done anything seditious under Roman law, and there's the end of the matter as Pilate sees it. In the presence of God's Light, he shows himself to be as blind as were the Pharisees who had hounded Jesus for healing a blind beggar on the Sabbath and whose leaders have now handed Jesus over to Pilate."*

Had Jesus claimed that he was the earthly king of the Jews, Pilate would have had grounds to convict Jesus, but Jesus was claiming to be a spiritual king, a king *"not of this world,"* and that was not a threat to Rome. Pilate may even have surmised that Jesus was delusional or crazy but that wouldn't have been a crime either so Pilate pronounces Jesus as innocent.

But then what happened? Just as all too often happens today, politics enters in and Pilate succumbs to political pressure. He doesn't want his boat rocked. He doesn't want to have a protest of uprising by the Pharisees, so he caves in and turns Jesus over for crucifixion, to end three years of problems caused by this pesky rabbi from Judea.

What Pilate doesn't realize, nor do the Pharisees, is that

the crucifixion in not the end of things; instead it is a coronation --- the placing of the King of Kings on his throne.

John of Patmos in our reading from Revelation describes Jesus allegorically on his throne as King of Kings. He is described as *"faithful witness," "first born of the dead"* and *"ruler of kings of the earth."*

These three titles each emphasize a distinctive theme of Christ's work and ministry --- the cross, the resurrection, and the ascension. The messianic king from the Davidic line is called *"my first born"* and *"faithful witness"* in the Psalms. In Colossians 1, Paul calls Jesus, *"the first born among the dead."* You can find other references in scripture to these three titles for the King of Kings.

Revelation 1 vividly portrays the manner and situation of the King of Kings', Christ's, coming. He will come with the clouds, everyone will see him including his executioners, and everyone on earth will moan because of him.

John of Patmos, in this verse, is drawing upon the Old Testament, Daniel 7:13 and Zechariah 12:10, which relate to the house of David and the inhabitants of Jerusalem but Revelation widens that to include everyone on earth in seeing Jesus' second coming.

The punch line is verse 8 of Revelation 1. *"I am the Alpha and the Omega, says the Lord God, who is, and who was, and who is to come, the Almighty."* (NIV)

Alpha and omega are letters of the Greek alphabet, alpha being the first letter and omega being the last. Here the verse equates God as the Alpha and the Omega but then switches to referring to Christ. God is the Alpha and the Omega, the first and the last, but so is Christ. This is a clear reference in my mind to the one God --- Father, Son and Holy Spirit. God came to earth as Jesus, in human form, and now reigns forever --- one God in three parts. This passage highlights God's eternal nature which has always been at work in human history and which will be at work forever.

The title "Almighty" in frequently used in the Old Testament to refer to God but, except in Revelation, is used only once in the New Testament (2 Corinthians 6:18). In Revelation it is used nine times and emphasizes sovereignty and dominion over all creation. It always refers to the one God, not specifically to Jesus.

John of Patmos in verse 6 states that Jesus made us to be a kingdom, and made us priests serving God and Father.

Being a servant to God is what we are charged to do until Jesus returns again in glory. This is Christ's final message to us as we come to the end of this church year.

Next week we enter a new church year and the annual season of Advent, the celebration of awaiting the coming of our Lord and Savior for the first time.

Today we are looking forward to his second coming, the glorious time when the King of Kings will come again.

Alleluia! Amen.

---

1. Lamar Williamson, Jr., <u>Preaching the Gospel of John</u>, Westminster John Knox Press, Louisville, 2004.

Part Two

Sermons for Other Sundays of the Christian Year (Ordinary Time)

The Wisdom of Children
James 3:13-4:3, 7-8a; Mark 9:30-37

There are several themes in today's two scripture passages from James and Mark. Egotism and pride are very evident as is greed. On the other hand, wisdom, child-like wisdom, is also there.

As I read these passages when I was preparing this message, I was in a brief quandary as to how to approach them. Should I talk about the negative aspects of human nature like egotism and greed, or should I talk about wisdom? I wasn't sure.

Both passages talk about selfish ambition. In the reading from James we are cautioned that people should show wisdom by their good life and by deeds done in humility. This is one kind of wisdom, human wisdom. The passage also talks about a second kind of wisdom, God's wisdom that comes from heaven, wisdom that is pure, considerate, submissive, impartial and sincere.

If we do not use wisdom, egotism and pride take over leading to selfish actions and, on occasion for some, violent actions which can lead to harm to others and to ourselves. The passage cautions us to submit to God and to resist egotism, pride and greed which come from the devil. The passage concludes, *"Come near to God and he will come near to you."* (NIV). Those who are wise will seek to become near to God.

Our scripture reading from Mark shows a lack of wisdom on the part of the disciples. Jesus has once again told them that he was going to be crucified yet they didn't understand and were too proud to ask him to explain.

Instead they argued among themselves about which one of them was the greatest. Their egotism had taken over and their pride was obscuring God's message.

One of my favorite parts of scripture in Proverbs 4:5-7. I like the New King James translation of this passage [1]: *"Get wisdom! Get understanding! Do not forget, nor turn away from the words of my mouth. Do not forsake her, and she will preserve you; Love her, and she will keep you. Wisdom is the principal thing; Therefore, get wisdom. And with all your getting, get understanding."* (NKJV)

Get wisdom! Get understanding! Wisdom is not knowledge. Knowledge is an accumulation of facts, an accumulation of information. Wisdom comes when these facts, that information, are understood and are applied in a peace-loving, considerate, and merciful way to do what is right in the sight of God. When one is full of egotism and pride, the heavenly form of wisdom is absent!

An anecdote I read recently tells of a young woman who asked for an appointment with her pastor to talk to him about a sin which worried her. When she saw him she said, "Pastor, I have become aware of a sin in my life which I cannot control. Every time I am in church I begin to look around at the other women, and I realize that I am the prettiest one in the whole congregation. None of the others can compare with my beauty. What can I do about this sin?"

The pastor replied, "Mary, that's not a sin, why that's just a mistake."

The woman was a prideful egotist. The pastor had wisdom.

Benjamin Franklin once said, *"There is perhaps no one of our natural passions so hard to subdue as pride. Beat it down, stifle it, mortify it as much as one pleases, it is still alive. Even if I could conceive that I had completely overcome it, I should probably be proud of my humility."*

Pride, greed, selfishness, egotism and all that go with them are hard to subdue. It takes great wisdom to keep them at bay.

Jesus cautioned the disciples that *"Anyone who wants to be first must be the very last, and the servant to all."* To do that one must exert great wisdom.

To drive home his point, Jesus took a child into his arms and said that one who *"... welcomes one of these little children in my name welcomes me; and whoever welcomes me does not welcome me but the one who sent me."* (NIV)

Lamar Williamson [2], a very prominent pastor and a member of the Presbytery of Western North Carolina, in discussing our scripture reading from Mark, said: *"Jesus reinforces his teaching on true greatness by an acted parable, identifying with a child... The force of Jesus' action hinges upon recognition of the low esteem in which children were held in the Greco-Roman world and realization that the Greek word used here for 'child' is the same as that used for the suffering servant of the Lord in Isaiah 53:2 ... Symbolically ... 'child' here applies to anyone who has need of help and more specifically to new disciples ... 'child' or 'little one' is a symbol for new followers of Jesus."*

The message is one of becoming a servant, not someone who is jockeying for position and honor.

The analogy of a child is a good one. Certainly children can be egotistic, greedy and prideful but they are born innocent and can be very wise, particularly when they are quite young.

Our daughter commented on her Facebook page that our then 2½ year old grandson patted her on her head and said, *"You nice Mommy."* That is true childlike wisdom.

Rev. Gary MacDonald, United Church of Canada, told the story of the wisdom of children in China. He was in the very poor rural area of Fujian Province one Christmas day. A friend took him to a small village church and he was surprised to find at the front of the church, together with the pastor and a small choir, an old man in red clothing with a fake white beard. Some small boys in front of him were very excited by the presence of this person. Rev. MacDonald asked them who he was and they were very surprised that he didn't know that he was the Old Man of Christmas.

Rev. MacDonald said that he played dumb and asked them to explain to him just who the Old Man of Christmas was. With wide eyes, they explained that the Old Man of Christmas was a kind man. He would give gifts to the children.

OK, nothing new here. The Santa Claus myth even seemed to have invaded this very poor village of rural China but here the story was different.

Rev. MacDonald thought that since the village was extremely poor, perhaps some group or individual had made a donation of toys for the children which the Old Man of Christmas would give to them later.

Yes, the children believed that they would receive gifts, but not the type of gifts Rev. MacDonald anticipated. They told him, *"If you go to sleep and are very still and quiet, the Old Man of Christmas will come to you. He will give you many gifts. He will put love in your heart. This is a special love you have for Mommy and Daddy. The Old Man of Christmas will make you clever. He will make you clever so that when you go over the mountain to school he will help you remember to be careful so that you do not fall and hurt yourself. The Old Man of Christmas will make you kind so that you help your teacher at school."*

Rev. MacDonald said that these were very poor children in a very poor village but that somehow he thought them to be rich.

These children were rich --- rich in wisdom. They were not burdened with pride, greed or egotism. They were the kind of children Jesus was referring to when he admonished his arguing disciples.

At the Pine Ridge, South Dakota, Red Cloud Indian School for Sioux children, a prayer is recited as follows:

"O Great Spirit, whose voice I hear in the woods, and whose breath gives life to all in the world, hear me! I am small and weak, I need your strength and wisdom. Let me walk in beauty, and make my eyes ever behold the red and purple sunset. Make my hands respect the things you have made and my ears sharp to hear your voice.

Make me wise so that I may understand the things you have taught my people. Let me learn the lessons you have hidden in every leaf and rock.

I seek strength, not to be greater than my brother, but to fight my greatest enemy — myself. Make me always ready to come to you with clean hands and straight eyes, so when life fades, as the fading sunset, my spirit may come to you without shame."

Amen!

1. Scripture taken from the New King James Version. Copyright © 1982 by Thomas Nelson, Inc., Used by permission. All rights reserved.
2. Lamar Williamson, Jr., <u>Mark: Interpretation, A Bible Commentary for Teaching and Preaching</u>, John Knox Press, Louisville, 1983

Talking to Children
Mark 9:30-37

The New Testament Lectionary readings for this Sunday are a portion of James 3 & 4 and Mark 9:30-37.

As I was thinking about today's sermon I was in a quandary as to which of the readings to select for today's sermon as both have strong messages for us.

The selection from James relates to what it means to have wisdom and how wisdom affects the choices that you make in your daily life.

The selection from Mark is a resurrection story, Christ's prediction of his betrayal and resurrection using a child as the object of the lesson that he is teaching his disciples.

It was almost a coin toss for me as to which of the two passages to discuss this morning.

I have served as the chaplain at Boy Scout Camp Bud Schiele in Rutherford County, NC for quite a few years. When I am at the camp I deal with hundreds of children and that annual experience made me opt for the passage from Mark.

While at the camp, for obvious reasons when dealing with hundreds of boys of all faiths, including many who are not Christian, I obviously can't preach to them about Jesus but I certainly can, and do, talk to them about God.

In our scripture reading Jesus was endeavoring to squelch the disciples' hankerings for greatness and used a child as an illustration of what it means to be great in the Kingdom of God. Today we at times romanticize our children. Those of us who are grandparents as I am are particularly prone to doing that, but back in Jesus' time that wasn't true. Children had no status, power or rights of any kind. They literally were not considered to be much more than property. They weren't full persons. For the most part they were dependent, vulnerable and unlearned. They were entirely subject to the authority of their father. Rabbis even grouped children with slaves, the feeble-minded, and the deaf. Children were considered to be insignificant. That is the context of Jesus' words to his disciples.

He has just told them once again that he would be betrayed, that he would be killed, and that he would rise again on the third day but they didn't understand and were afraid to ask him to explain.

Isn't that what children often do? They hear something that an adult tells them, they don't understand, or in some cases don't want to understand, and they are afraid to ask for an explanation. Hopefully when I talk to the boys at the Scout Camp about God, they do understand. I think that most of them do, but I know that many will not understand everything I say and won't ask. That is just the way children are. But so are many adults.

Children also often are jockeying with each other for recognition and are competing with each other for status. I see that with Scouts that I call "badge hounds." They do everything possible to accumulate more and more awards and patches to sew onto their uniform sashes to show off how great they are, or how great they think they are. That is a sign of immaturity and desire for recognition and it isn't limited to children. Adults also have this tendency. I know Scout leaders who cover their uniforms with all manner of patches and awards and who seem to be on an endless quest to receive more and more things to attach to their uniforms. They are like the squabbling disciples in our scripture reading.

Who is the greatest among us? Who will get to sit at the right hand of Christ in the Kingdom?

William Barclay [1] commented that the squabbling, *"... shows how far the disciples were from realizing the real meaning of Jesus' Messiah-ship ... Repeatedly he has told them what awaited him in Jerusalem and yet they were still thinking of his Kingdom in earthly terms and of themselves as his chief ministers of state. There is something heart-breaking in the thought of Jesus going towards a Cross and his disciples arguing about who would be the greatest."*

But when Jesus asked them, *"... what they had been arguing about they had nothing to say. It was the silence of shame ... So long as they thought that Jesus was not listening and that Jesus had not seen, the argument about who should be greatest seemed fair enough* [to them], *but when that argument had to be stated in the presence of Jesus it was seen in all its unworthiness."* Jesus had to sit the disciples down and teach them, telling them that greatness in his Kingdom could only be found, not by being masters but by being servants of all.

Barclay went on to say, *"The really great persons, the people who are remembered as having made a real contribution to life, are the people who said to themselves not, 'How can I use ... society to further my own prestige and my own personal ambitions?' but, 'How can I use my personal gifts and talents to serve others?'*

"Every economic problem would be solved if people lived for what they could do for others and not for what they could get for themselves. Every political problem would be solved if the ambition of people was to serve others and not to enhance their own prestige. The divisions and disputes which tear the church and society asunder would for the most part never occur if only the desire of people was to serve without caring what position they occupied. When Jesus spoke to the supreme greatness and value of a person whose ambition was to be a servant, he laid down one of the greatest practical truths in the world."

That is what I try to teach the children at the Scout Camp and what I hope to impart on you each Sunday.

Amen

1. William Barclay, The Gospel of Mark, rev. ed., Westminster John Knox Press, Louisville, KY, 1975 (Quotes have been rephrased or paraphrased to make them gender neutral).

Give Thanks: Surrender to the Grace of God
Mark 13:1-8

In the December 2008 issue of *National Geographic Magazine*, there was a feature story entitled "Herod: The Holy Land's Greatest Builder." If you subscribe to *National Geographic* you may remember that article which talked about the magnificent palace that Herod had built for himself, but more importantly, it talked about the great Temple which he built in Jerusalem on the Temple Mount.

Herod was born around 73 BC and grew up in Judea. He saw the benefit of working with the Romans. He was considered to have betrayed the Jewish people but he strove to reconcile the demands of the Romans with those of the Jews. He walked a very thin tightrope and when he was made king by the Romans, Judea had two decades of relative economic prosperity and peace. He had no compunction however about crushing those who threatened his rule and he even drowned his wife's brother out of fear that he might usurp Herod's throne.

During his reign, Herod undertook massive construction projects one of which was rebuilding the Second Temple. Solomon had built the First Temple after the death of King David. That Temple lasted from the 10th century BC until it was burned by Nebuchadnezzar in about 586 BC when the Babylonians captured Judea. It is not absolutely certain what happened to the Ark of the Covenant which was in the Temple but it is believed that it too was burned by the Babylonians.

About 50 years later in 538 BC, Cyrus the Great permitted the Jews to return from Babylonian exile with the temple vessels and Zerubbabel built the Second Temple to replace Solomon's Temple. It was completed in 515 BC.

When Herod came to power in 37 BC he was determined to please his Jewish subjects and also to show off his leadership to the Romans by making the temple bigger and better than it had ever been. He built what was considered to be indestructible but it wasn't, just as the Titanic was not unsinkable.

Herod greatly enlarged the Temple with massive stonework, magnificent porches, double and triple arches, and more. The foundation stones were huge, some more than 40 feet long weighing more than 600 tons. All that remains today is the Western Wall, the so-called "Wailing Wall," Judaism's most sacred place. On it rests the Dome of the Rock, Islam's third holiest site.

In our scripture, the disciples are seeing the Temple, most likely for the first time. They are awed by it and by the massive size of its stones. In their eyes it would stand forever. It was incredibly well built. It was a monument to God.

For the Jews, the Temple was the symbol of God's presence and was God's earthly home.

During the Exodus, the Ark of the Covenant was kept in a tent. That tent to the Jews was God's home at that time. Solomon built the first real home for God and now with Herod's construction there was a glorious new home. It was truly great but Jesus astonished the disciples --- he told them that the impossible would happen. The Temple would fall.

That was unthinkable. The Jews believed that without the Temple, God would be gone. God would leave them.

But Jesus said no. God would still be there. Jesus told them that there would be very real threats to people --- false prophets, wars, famine and earthquakes. But he told them not to be worried, not to be scared --- everything was part of a bigger plan.

We don't know if Mark's words were written before or after the Romans destroyed the Temple in 70 AD but that isn't important. Mark is quoting Christ's words, not using hindsight. The Temple would fall and all sorts of disasters would happen.

What would we think today if we were told that everything important to our faith, our country, our very way of life would be turned upside down?

This is what Jesus was telling the disciples, but he also said, don't worry. God is still in control. The reality is that the only thing they or we today can count on in life is God.

Rather than looking around and trying to define God by what happens in this world, we must face what we believe about this world with the hope and confidence that God is working it all out.

Sometimes what seems like bad news might really be good news if we just filter it through God. A good friend or family member might be critically ill and be suffering and die. We look at that as bad news but it really is good news. That person no longer suffers and is now with God.

There is evil in this world but God doesn't cause it or inflict pain on us. No matter what happens we can trust that God holds us and ultimately God will take care of us. Nothing that happens in this world or in our lives can take away the fact that God is in control.

We need to surrender to God, not to hold on to earthly things. The Israelites were holding on to the Temple, a thing built by man, Herod in this case, a thing which wasn't God's home but rather was blinding them to God.

What are our temples?

The Temple effectively was an idol. Its destruction by the Romans brought real focus on God, not on huge stones piled upon each other. Without the Temple, people learned that God and Christ were in charge.

Several years ago an email was being passed around from one pastor to another. It told of a certain pastor's experiences on a long airplane flight.

This pastor was returning home from a church conference. The first warning of possible problems was when the fasten seat belt sign came on. The ride became bumpy due to turbulence. Then, after a brief time, a calm voice over the intercom said, "We shall not be serving beverages as we are experiencing some turbulence. Please make sure that your seat belt is securely fastened."

As the pastor looked around the aircraft, it was obvious that many passengers were apprehensive, just as I have been in similar circumstances. Then the voice on the intercom apologized that meal service was being discontinued. Very severe turbulence was just ahead. Then the storm broke. Ominous cracks of thunder were so loud that they could be heard over the roar of the jet engines. Lightning began to flash all around the airplane.

The plane was tossed about like a cork in a turbulent ocean. One moment the plane was lifted on terrific currents of air. The next, it dropped as if it were about to crash.

The pastor confessed his discomfort and fear with those around him and said that, as he looked around, it was clear that nearly all of the passengers were upset and alarmed. Some were praying. Things seemed ominous. Many were wondering if they would make it through the storm.

Then the pastor noticed a little girl. The storm seemed meaningless to her. She had her feet tucked beneath her as she was calmly reading a book. Everything within her small world was calm and orderly. Sometimes she closed her eyes and dozed off. Then she would awaken and read again, straightening her legs. It seemed that worry and fear were not in her world.

When the plane was being buffeted by the terrible storm --- when it lurched this way and that --- when it rose and fell with frightening severity --- when all of the adults were scared half to death --- that marvelous child was completely composed and unafraid. The minister could not believe his eyes.

It was not surprising that when the plane finally landed safely at its destination, and all the passengers were hurrying to disembark, the pastor lingered to speak to the girl he had watched for such a long time. Having commented about the storm and the behavior of the plane, he asked her why she hadn't been afraid. The child simply replied, "Because my daddy is the pilot and he is taking me home."

The storms of our lives can cause us to lose our perspective. We need to remember that our Father is the pilot, so don't worry. He is in control and is taking us home. Even if the temples fall down around us, if our family fails us, if the church catches fire and burns to the ground, if disaster strikes the country, we still have all we need for our Father is in control. He is piloting our lives. That is the kind of faith we need --- the kind that says when bad things happen, we will be OK because God knows the big picture.

There are wars and rumors of war, there are natural disasters, there are things that threaten our way of life every day, but the ultimate truth is still there. Don't be alarmed for if we endure to the end, if we surrender to the grace of God, then we will be saved.

Alleluia! Amen.

Living a Servant Life
Ruth 1:1-18

Our Scripture lesson is from one of the shortest books of the Bible, the Book of Ruth. There are only four chapters in the book taking up only three or four pages in the Bible, yet this short Old Testament book tells a remarkable story about a remarkable woman, Ruth.

Ruth was a Moabite, not a Jew. She was the daughter-in-law of Naomi.

Naomi, her husband, and their two sons had fled from Bethlehem because of a severe famine and went to live in Moab, hoping for a better life. The two sons married Moabite women, Orpha and Ruth, and for a while things seemed to be going well.

As an aside, Oprah Winfrey was named for Orpha but, due to a spelling error on her birth certificate, Orpha was changed to Oprah. The original Orpha is not often mentioned or recalled. But for an error in modern times her name would have become a household word.

In any event, going back to our Old Testament story, Naomi's husband Elimelech died leaving Naomi a widow. A widow's lot in life back then was very poor but Naomi still had her two sons and their wives to care for her, at least she did for a short while.

As fate would have it, both sons died. We don't know how or why. Scripture doesn't tell us. The result was that all three women were widows and were in dire straits. Naomi had little choice but to return to Bethlehem where she had family who might assist her, so she set out for home.

Naomi had fled Bethlehem because of famine and now she had to return. There was nothing for her in Moab. The name "Bethlehem" literally means "house of bread." It is ironic that Naomi and her family had fled from there in the first place. The house of plenty had failed them.

But now Naomi was returning. Her Moabite daughters-in-law initially started out with her but Naomi stopped and told them to stay in Moab where they had family. They were both still young, probably in their twenties, and they might find new husbands if they stayed. Because they were not Jews and were foreigners, their chances of finding husbands in Bethlehem were very slight. Staying was totally logical for them. Today we would call it a no-brainer. Orpha did stay but Ruth did not. She would not leave Naomi. She left her homeland, went with Naomi and ventured to a new country with a totally different culture and people who worshipped one God, not the gods that Moabites worshipped. Could you do that? Walk away from everything you had ever known including your religious traditions?

Why did Ruth do that? She too was a widow. She would have few prospects for a good life in Bethlehem. Her chances would have been far better in Moab but, nevertheless, she went with Naomi. She was all that Naomi had. She went to support Naomi as best she could and to do whatever was necessary to help her. Ruth willingly accepted a servant life, a life of being a servant to Naomi.

Naomi had no hope of remarrying and having children at her age. She was probably in her forties or older. Ruth might well have been giving up any chance to remarry. Things did not look good for either woman.

In antiquity, widowhood was hazardous. Women had very little opportunity to be independent. They depended upon their fathers, husbands and sons for support. Often, if a widow did not have such support, she might have to sell herself into slavery, resort to prostitution, or else starve to death. There weren't many options for widows.

So here were two widows headed for Bethlehem, one returning home, and the other, a young woman hoping to be able to support the older woman.

What happened after that? The gist of the story is that Ruth supports Naomi by gleaning grain in farmers' fields. It was the custom for farmers to leave a bit of wheat or barley in the fields for the benefit of the poor to scratch out a meager living. Ruth's gathering of this grain is what sustained the two widows. It was a hard servant's life indeed.

Like a fairy tale, the story ends happily ever after. Ruth meets Boaz, a kindly farmer and a distant relative of Naomi. He instructs his field hands to leave an extra bit of grain for Ruth to glean. Eventually, Boaz marries Ruth and all ends well. Ruth gives birth to a son, Obed. Obed becomes the father of Jesse, the father of David. Ruth's return to Bethlehem with Naomi results in the lineage of David and eventually to Jesus. One servant life leads directly to the ultimate servant life in all of history.

What is a servant life? Do many people live a true servant life? Do you know anyone who has done so?

Look around you in the sanctuary. Look around and everyone you can see is in one way of another a servant – a servant to others and a servant to God. I want to single out one women as an example of true dedication to a servant life. She was among the most dedicated servants of the Lord that I have ever known. One person can do an incredible amount to help others and to do the work of God. Those that do often don't get recognized for their efforts – nor do they expect to be recognized. They do it for love – love of God and love of others.

This phenomenal lady in Lenoir, North Carolina was Dr. Jane Carswell Roberts. Dr. Carswell was a beloved family practice physician in Lenoir for many years. She retired and has since passed away but mention her name on the street in Lenoir, North Carolina and almost anyone will know who she is. Why? It is because retirement did not slow her down. She always contributed virtually every waking minute to serving others. She was a Ruling Elder at the Fairview Presbyterian Church and went overboard in her service to that congregation. She was the prime-mover in the construction of Shelter Home, a refuge for battered women and their children. She spent innumerable hours working at the "Pay It Forward" food pantry counseling and praying with and for those who came to the food pantry for assistance. She annually organized an ecumenical multi-racial worship service in December, an outgrowth of reconciliation efforts following a race riot during the time of the civil rights crisis. Dr. Carswell seemed to have her hands and support in a multitude of other community service programs. She was a true servant of God.

We all know others who are also true servants God. When you see them and talk to them, thank them for all that they do but don't stop there. Get involved in their efforts and join them as true servants of God. It is easy to say what a great job someone is doing. It is a lot harder to follow their example, but do it! That is what God expects of you.

Amen.

Watching and Waiting
Matthew 25:14-30

Each week as I prepare to write a sermon, I look at the suggested scripture readings for the day. Then I think about these suggestions and what they say, I choose one or more of the readings, and then start to compose my thoughts about the selected scripture. I have a very extensive library of theological material, including sermons given by other pastors. I have it all on a spreadsheet and can quickly search to see what resources I have which may be relevant to the scripture that I have chosen.

We all know the Parable of the Talents from Matthew 25. It is familiar so presumably I should have a lot of information in my files about it. Right? **Wrong!** There is absolutely nothing there.

Why would that be the case? The reason most probably is the timing of this particular scripture reading in the church calendar. It falls in November when most churches are conducting their annual pledge drives and pastors are encouraging their congregations to increase their giving if at all possible.

In most Bible translations, the parable is called the Parable of the Talents. In the NIV translation, it is called the Parable of the Bags of Gold --- but it is not about money. It is about the responsible stewardship of God's gifts. There is a big difference between the two. Nevertheless, the two are easily confused which is probably why so few pastors preach on this parable at this time of year.

That said, the parable's message is really one of watching and waiting for Jesus' return and in being good stewards of all that he has given to us, our talents.

Biblically, in monetary terms, the bags of money, the talents, were huge amounts of money. A talent was a measure of weight, not a unit of currency or a coin, although it is true that later a coin was minted which was called a talent. The two are not the same thing.

The talents mentioned in the parable were approximately equal in value to seventy-five pounds of silver worth about 6000 denarii, or about $247,200, nearly a quarter of a million dollars. Thus the landowner in the parable gave his servants close to two million dollars to invest in his absence.

The analogy to talents as we understand the word today is that the three servants varied greatly in their innate talent to do things, just as each of us varies in our talents. God has given each and every one of us different talents and expects us to make the most of those talents. Some of us have talents as teachers or farmers or railroad workers or auto mechanics or other things. I was blessed with talents in science and engineering and think that I was reasonably good at using those talents. But my talents as a farmer are hopeless. I can grow weeds but not much else.

God gave each of us talents and expects us to use those talents to the best of our ability for the benefit of his kingdom. That is what the Parable of the Talents is telling us.

The landowner who is going on the journey is Jesus. He is going to the Father, but he will return. In his absence he expects each of us to use the talents that have been given to us in the furtherance of his kingdom. The three servants each have different talents, just as each of us does. How well we manage our talents is up to each of us and when Christ returns we will be judged on our stewardship of what was given to us.

The servant who was given five talents in the parable probably set up some kind of business and made a large and profitable capital investment. In terms of talents as we understand the word today, he might be a great theologian such as Dietrich Bonhoeffer, the great German Lutheran pastor who staunchly opposed Adolph Hitler and his Nazi dictatorship. He might be someone like Albert Einstein who developed the theory of relativity, a pillar of modern physics. These two men and hundreds of other men and women used their talents for the benefit of everyone and continued to do so throughout their lives.

The servant who was given two talents perhaps reflects most of us more closely. We aren't Einsteins or Bonhoeffers but most of us have done our best with the talents we were given and, even if we are retired from our life's work, we continue to serve the Lord through volunteer activity.

The third servant, who was given one talent, might be called lazy or over cautious. He was afraid of doing anything with what he had been given and he hid it while awaiting his master's return.

Do you know anyone like that? I am sure that you do. But, you might ask, "What's wrong with his being cautious?" Isn't discretion a virtue? Isn't caution? Isn't carefulness?

Quoting Walter Brueggemann, et al [1], *"... with this third servant virtues became vices. Prudence and wariness easily became self-protectiveness and restraint. Inhibition turns to fear and the servant ends up refusing the risk of trading in the market place. By preserving exactly what had been entrusted to him he can at least minimally stay in the good graces of his master — or so he thinks."*

Note that in the parable, the master says to the first two servants, *"Well done good and faithful servant!"* Each is given praise and greater responsibilities, just as each of us is expected to continue in our service to the Lord and to magnify that service as best we can.

The third servant is called wicked and lazy. Like many modern counterparts, he did nothing with his talent. He will not be looked upon with favor at the time of judgment.

As an aside, did you note the joke in the master's comments to him? *"You should have put my money on deposit with the bankers, so that when I returned I would have received it back with interest."*

In those times Jews avoided charging interest to each other. The reference to interest may well be a suggestion that he should have invested the money with gentiles.

"To the one choosing security over risk, the Lord remains a hard master, one who seems to reap where he does not sow and gather where he has not planted. Fearfulness breeds more fear. The prospect of joy and the freedom of response are gone. But those who risk discover a Lord ready to share the delight of his presence and participation in his mission. They discover a link with the teller of the story, who knows all about risks and whose love is neither prudent nor calculating." [1]

Amen!

---

(1) Walter Brueggemann, et al, <u>Texts for Preaching – Year A</u>, Westminster John Knox Press, Louisville, KY, 1995.

Our God of Love
Romans 10:8b-14

I have some difficult questions to raise with you this morning, questions which have long concerned me as a Christian and a pastor.

Is accepting Jesus Christ as your Lord and Savior the only way to achieve salvation? If so, what about the billions of people over history who have never heard about Jesus Christ and the many millions who lived and died before the time of Christ. Are they doomed to Hell for all eternity?

Millions of people live lives that are admirable and caring but do not worship Jesus and billions more have never had the opportunity to know about Christ.

Personally, I cannot believe that a loving God would ignore these people and treat them in the same way that Adolph Hitler or Osama bin Laden might be treated. Our God is a God of love and compassion, not a God of vengeance. How then can we say that non-believers are cast out from any possibility for salvation?

Does our God of love not love all of humankind, Christians and non-Christians alike? I believe that he does. Christ didn't put any limits on his love and forgiveness. Why then would God?

Our epistle reading from Paul's letter to the Romans says, *"No one who believes in him will be put to shame. For there is no distinction between Jew and Greek: the same Lord is Lord of all and is generous to all who call on him. For, everyone who calls on the name of the Lord will be saved."* (NRSV)

OK, that much is clear. If you accept and follow Jesus, the Christ, you will be saved by grace. **Period**. End of report.

But is that really all? Can others be saved? 1 John 2:2, in referring to Jesus, suggests that they can with the words, *"... he is the atoning sacrifice for our sins, and not for ours only but also for the sins of the whole world."* (NRSV). Remember the thief who was crucified along with Jesus? He was not a believer. He knew that Jesus was a good man who had been unfairly convicted. D. L. Moody [1] said, *"The thief had nails through both hands, so that he could not work; and a nail through each foot, so that he could not run errands for the Lord; he could not lift a hand or a foot toward his salvation, and yet Christ offered him the gift of God; and he took it. Christ threw him a passport and took him into paradise."*

Our epistle passage from Romans goes on to ask, *"But how are they to call on one in whom they have not believed? And how are they to believe in one of whom they have never heard? And how are they to hear without someone to proclaim him?"* (NRV). These are the same questions that I am asking. How can these people be saved?

In his best-selling book *Love Wins* [2], Rob Bell asked if only a select few people would make it to heaven and if all of the others would end up suffering forever in hell. He also asked if God would find that to be acceptable.

How could a loving God ever do this?

How could God ever allow something as terrifying as that to occur --- banning untold millions to suffer in agony forever?

Further if only a select few people would go to heaven, on what basis would they be chosen? Blind luck? By the spin of a roulette wheel or toss of the dice? Because of where they were born or who their family was?

Is our God like that?

Would our God permit that?

These are disturbing questions.

Can a person live a life of charity and concern for others, a life unblemished by hate or crime, a life of unbounded love for humankind, and not receive salvation because he or she never knew Christ or never had the opportunity to know Christ? In other words, a person like Mahatma Gandhi, or like Siddhartha Gautama, the founder of Buddhism, or like so many others.

Would our God of Love do that to them? Would they all go to Hell, if there is a Hell, and if so, what is Hell?

We picture Hell as a place run by Satan who marches around with a pitchfork pushing people into fires where they scream out in agony for all eternity. Is that what Hell is? I don't think so and neither does Rob Bell.

If you go back to the Old Testament scriptures, you won't find any such description of Hell other than brief words that refer to death and the grave. You will find the Hebrew word "Sheol" referring to a mysterious place where people go when they die. Other brief references simply refer to the realm of the dead – no fires, no agony, no pitchforks, no devils. The Bible really doesn't tell us what Hell is like.

In the New Testament, Jesus refers to hell fires but what is he talking about? The Greek word that is translated into Hell in the New Testament is "Gehenna", literally meaning "Valley of Hinnom", an actual valley near Jerusalem. This valley was the city dump for Jerusalem, a trash heap that was kept burning in order to get rid of the trash. Gehenna was the town's garbage pile so, in the context of Jesus' days, going to Hell literally meant being thrown out with the garbage. Jesus was most likely using the garbage dump allegorically as referring to death with little or no hope of salvation or resurrection.

The New Testament also uses the word "Hades" but this is simply the Greek word for the Hebrew "Sheol", the place of the dead – no fires, no pitchforks, no eternal agony – just death.

So what can we conclude from scripture? Going to Hell simply seems to refer to dying without salvation. **Period.**

If that is the case, does anyone have hope of salvation if they never accepted Christ or didn't have the opportunity to do so? C. S. Lewis seems to think that they do. In an interview back is 1963 he said, *"There are many different ways of bringing people into His Kingdom, even some ways I specifically dislike."* (Quoted in *His*, November, 1976)

How is this possible? Grace answers the question for us Christians but is there hope for non-Christians and for those who died with no knowledge of Christ. Is grace available to them?

I certainly hope so. I don't think that a loving God would treat Gandhi, Hitler and bin Laden in the same way. Gandhi personified goodness; Hitler and bin Laden personified evil.

Our epistle reading raises the question of what happens to those who don't know Jesus. Further in Romans 11, referring to persons who lived long before the time of Christ, we find the words, *"So too at the present time there is a remnant, chosen by grace. But if it is by grace, it is no longer on the basis of works, otherwise grace would no longer be grace."* (NRSV). **There you have it.** This passage refers to the period long before Christ and to the fact that God's grace was available to others.

Why then do some Christians believe that salvation is only for Christians and, in some cases, only for those of a specific denomination? Those conclusions come from misinterpretation of the words of Jesus and the New Testament writers, words which at times are not accurate translations of the original Greek and Hebrew writings.

Consider Paul's letter to the Galatians, chapter 2, verse 16: *"... we know that a person is justified not by the works of the law but through faith in Jesus Christ."* (NRSV). Sounds totally clear doesn't it? But is it? The words *"in Jesus Christ"* have another meaning in the original Greek. Often Greek words have multiple meanings depending upon the context in which they are used. The second meaning is *"of Jesus Christ"*, not *"in Jesus Christ."* In this context grace results through the faith **of** Jesus Christ, not through faith **in** Jesus Christ. Which interpretation is correct? I don't know and I leave it to you to decide for yourself.

Remember however that time after time in the Old Testament, we read of God's anger with the Israelites and his inevitable forgiveness. The God of Abraham, Isaac and Jacob is indeed a God of love, not vengeance. Rob Bell [(2)] outlined three different viewpoints on this issue:

First is the belief that Jesus is the only way and that if you don't accept him as Lord and Savior you are going to Hell.

Second is the belief that salvation is open to everyone, no matter what their faith tradition is. Bell suggests that there are multiple ways in which one can achieve salvation.

Third is that the Jesus' love is so all embracing, that everyone of any faith tradition, Hindus, Buddhists, Muslims, Shintoists and all others will be included.

Many Christians are very uneasy at this latter suggestion. They react by accusing anyone who suggests it that they are claiming that Jesus doesn't matter, that Christianity is meaningless, that the cross is irrelevant, that what you believe is not important. **This is absolutely not true. Salvation is indeed available to everyone, Christian or not. It is Christ's decision. We as Christians belong to Christ. Christ does not belong to us. Christ can save anyone whom he chooses.**

The Rev. Mike Johnston, my co-pastor when I was at First Presbyterian in Bessemer City, NC said, *"... we as Christians belong to Jesus Christ, having been enjoined by him through baptism, but Jesus does not belong to us. We are his, he is not ours! That is something all too often forgotten by many well intended preachers. We are the Lord's, to be sure; so where did we get the notion that Jesus' statement that he is the way, the truth and the life pertain exclusively to Christians?*

"... Jesus has said, 'I have another sheep not of this fold.' Jesus has the freedom to call whomever he chooses, however he chooses, whenever he chooses, even if they may not know it. This answers the nagging question about

the person of another faith tradition who leads a holy life, who is clearly in contact with the living God but does not confess Jesus as Lord and Savior."

What Jesus does is declare that he alone is saving everybody.

He leaves the door way, way open.

I hope and trust that the door is open wide enough for Gandhi and for all good people everywhere, Christian or not.

I can't believe that our loving God and Savior would have it any other way.

Amen.

---

1. Emma Moody Fitt, ed. <u>Day by Day with D. L. Moody</u>, Moody Press, Chicago, 1977
2. Rob Bell, <u>Love Wins</u>, Harper-Collins, New York, 2011

Note: Scripture quotations in this sermon are from the New Revised Standard Version of the Bible, copyright 1989, by the Division of Christian Education of the National Council of Churches of Christ in the U. S. A. Used by permission. All rights reserved.

This sermon was preached at the Trinity Presbyterian Church in Prescott, AZ, July 31, 2016

The Greatest Commandment
Matthew 22:34-46

In an effort to trap Jesus into saying something that would justify their charging him with heresy, the scribes and priests, the Pharisees and the Sadducees, asked him *"By what authority are you doing these things, and who gave you the authority?"* They were hoping that Jesus would answer them in a manner which was contrary to the rules, at least the rules as they interpreted them. They wanted a good reason to get rid of this pesky rabbi from Nazareth. Matthew 21:23 through 22:22 describes how Jesus responded. I urge you to read the full story in Matthew 21 and 22 to refresh your mind about this part of scripture.

Jesus countered the Pharisees' questions with three parables – the Parable of the Two Sons, the Parable of the Wicked Vineyard Tenants, and the Parable of the Wedding Party. All three parables were clear attacks on the scribes and priests, each parable depicting them as not serving God, but instead serving their own selfish ends.

Then they tried another way to entrap Jesus, this time by trying to get him to answer the question if it was lawful (meaning Jewish law) to pay taxes to the emperor or not. They hoped that he would answer in a way which would get the Romans on their side against Jesus.

Again, Jesus thwarted their rather obvious ploy. He responded, *"So give back to Caesar what is Caesar's and to God what is God's"* (NIV). That response cut the Pharisees off at the knees and they left and ended the discussion, at least for the time being. However, they were far from finished. They were not giving up.

Once the Pharisees left, scripture tells us in Matthew 22:23-33 that the other Jewish leadership group, the Sadducees, picked up the assault on Jesus with questions about resurrection. The Sadducees, unlike the Pharisees, did not believe in resurrection and they hoped to trap Jesus somehow in a heretical answer. Jesus silenced the Sadducees very forcefully – so much so that according to Matthew 22:33 the crowd that witnessed Jesus' exchange with the Sadducees *"were astonished at his teaching."*

The *Adult Bible Studies* for the Presbyterian Church USA Sunday school in 2013 commented that, *"The common people heard*

(Jesus) and ... found a power and conviction in him that they did not find in their conventional leaders." They saw what the Pharisees and Sadducees did not see.

Jesus' oral defeat of the Sadducees caused the Pharisees to reinitiate their attempts to entrap Jesus. Our gospel reading makes that clear with the words, *"When the Pharisees heard that he had silenced the Sadducees, they gathered together and one of them, a lawyer, asked him a question to test him."* (NIV).

It would be well at this point to briefly explain the difference between Sadducees, Pharisees and lawyers in the time of Christ. The Sadducees and Pharisees were the political parties of the day. The Sadducees were responsible for the care and upkeep of the Temple in Jerusalem and were the Priesthood, which was the highest social class in Judean society. They rejected any belief in resurrection and in oral law. They saw the Torah, the Pentateuch, as the sole source of divine authority. Unless these first five books of the Bible stated it, it was not a valid interpretation of scriptural law.

The Pharisees, on the other hand, did believe in resurrection and did not see the Torah as the sole source of divine authority. Rather they supported oral tradition, the so called "Oral Torah" that had been handed down over the centuries, in addition to the written Torah. They believed that God had given Moses knowledge of what the laws meant and how they should be applied. In other words, an Oral Torah. The *Jewish Virtual Library* says that the Pharisees were, *"... in a sense blue-collar Jews who adhered to the tenets developed after the destruction of (Solomon's) Temple, that is such things as individual prayer and assembly in synagogues."*

The Sadducees were "strict constructionists." If the written Torah didn't say it, it wasn't so. Period!

The Sanhedrin, the Jewish Supreme Council, was made up of 71 members, both Sadducees and Pharisees, and their responsibility was to interpret civil and religious laws. As you can see, they were as different as our Democrat and Republican Parties are today. They disagreed on many things but one thing they agreed on was the need to get Jesus and his followers out of their collective hair.

Going back to our scripture reading, the Sadducees had backed off and the Pharisees resumed their attack on Jesus by having a lawyer present the ultimate question to Jesus, "Which commandment in the law is the greatest." Lawyers in first century

Israel were also theologians because the law of Israel was the Torah. What the Pharisees were doing was sending an expert, someone trained in the law, to outmaneuver Jesus.

You need to remember that the Torah contains 613 commandments, not just the 10 we Christians normally think about and here was a lawyer asking Jesus, "Of the 613 commandments, which one is the most important." In the lawyer's eyes, Jesus had only one chance in 613 of getting the answer right. Those are lousy odds in anyone's book.

How did Jesus respond? He said, *"Love the Lord your God with all your heart, and with all your soul, and with all your mind."* But he didn't stop there. He continued by saying, *"This is the first and greatest commandment. And the second is like it: 'Love your neighbor as yourself.' All the Law and the prophets hang on these two commandments."* (NIV).

Jesus gave two commandments, not one, in answer to the question, and concluded with the statement that these two commandments encompassed the totality of the law.

Frederick Buechner, a noted theologian, in his book <u>Listening to Your Life</u> [1], wrote a rather tongue in cheek commentary on Jesus' response. Buechner commented that a lawyer wanted Jesus to define what he meant by a neighbor. Was a neighbor a Jew? Was the neighbor someone who lived close to you? Someone who lived in your town? Is one mile close enough? Three miles? Ten miles? How close should you live to someone to consider him to be a neighbor?

Jesus responded by telling the lawyer the Parable of the Good Samaritan (Luke 10:25-37) and effectively defined a neighbor as anyone, anywhere who was in need.

Jesus answered the question asked by quoting a part of Deuteronomy 6:4-5, *"Hear, O Israel: The Lord our God is one. Love the Lord your God with all your heart and with all your soul and with all your strength"* Jesus quoted the Torah, the written law. What he quoted is known as the "Shema" or "Shema Yisrael", the first words of a section of the Torah which is recited by faithful Jews at morning and evening services. Jesus quoted the Shema and then he added the second commandment, *"...love your neighbor as yourself"* from Leviticus 19:18, another part of the Torah. Jesus responded to the lawyer and the Pharisees by throwing their law right back at them and by confounding them with a question of his own, *"What do you think about the Messiah? Whose son is he?"* They replied, *"The son of David."* Jesus asks then for the Pharisees to explain how the

Messiah could be the son of David if David calls the Messiah "Lord". Would anyone call their son Lord? Hardly. Not even in England's House of Lords could that happen. Lordship passes from father to son, not the other way around. We refer to God as Lord and to Jesus as Lord – the father and the son – not the son only. The Pharisees could not respond to Jesus' question and as our text says, *"No one was able to give him an answer, nor from that day did anyone dare to ask him any more questions."* (NIV).

The point of Jesus' answers to the questions asked of him is that the entirety of the Ten Commandments is encompassed in loving God with all your heart, soul and mind and in loving your neighbor as yourself.

The first four of the Ten Commandments are reflected in loving God –
#1 You shall have no other gods.
#2 You shall not make idols and worship them.
#3 You shall not take God's name in vain.
#4 You shall keep the Sabbath day holy.

Loving your neighbor as yourself obviously includes:
#5 Honoring your parents.
#6 Not committing murder.
#7 Not committing adultery.
#8 Not stealing.
#9 Not bearing false witness.
#10 Not coveting anything of your neighbor's.

You need not memorize the Ten Commandments. You only need to remember two – loving God and loving your neighbor as yourself, and remembering that your neighbor is anyone in need, including your enemies.

That is not easy to do at times but that is what being a Christian means. We worship one Messiah, one God, one Lord, a God and Lord in three parts, Father, Son and Holy Spirit, a God who commands us to love our neighbors as ourselves.

Amen!

---

1. Frederick Buechner, "Neighbor – July 27", <u>Listening to Your Life</u>, Harper Collins, New York, 1992

Why Are We Afraid of Evangelism?
Isaiah 60:1-5a; Acts 9:1-19

One of the most effective ways to bring people to Christ is to talk to them about God and about what your faith means to you. Telling people what we believe, and why, does indeed bring people to Christ. Why are so many Christians afraid to do it?

Our scripture reading from Isaiah 60 begins, *"Arise, shine, for your light has come, and the glory of the Lord rises upon you."* (NIV). That light has risen upon each and every one of us but do we ever tell others about it? The answer to that question, I fear, is "no" or "not often enough."

Our scripture reading from Acts is perhaps the most dramatic conversion story in the Bible. Here is Paul, a man dedicated to the destruction of Christianity, who encounters Christ on a country road, is struck down and is blinded. Paul had a real problem.

Three days later Jesus sends Ananias to Paul. Ananias reluctantly restores Paul's sight. He tells the Lord that Paul had come to arrest believers but Jesus replies, *"Go! This man is my chosen instrument to proclaim my name to the Gentiles and their kings and to the people of Israel."* (NIV).

Paul was dramatically converted to the faith but the Lord did not want it to end there. His plan was for Paul to become his evangelist, and indeed Paul did. He traveled the world telling anyone who would listen of his conversion story and of the story of Christ. He did this tirelessly and the result was the explosive growth of Christianity. Paul's story made an incredible difference and so can our individual faith stories.

Certainly none of us has a story anywhere near as compelling as Paul's, but we all do have a story and our personal story can bring others to the faith --- not by the hundreds or thousands as Paul's story did, but one or two at a time.

When we talk to people, particularly when there are times of transition in their lives – weddings, birth of children, serious illnesses, times of major concern, or the passing or funerals of friends or loved ones --- these are the times when people are receptive to hearing about Christ.

Similarly, when you are engaged in community service,

particularly when it is supported by the church, tell those you deal with how Christ motivates you and ask them if they would like to participate in these activities. If they indicate interest, tell them what the church does in the community and the many mission activities that the church supports. Invite them to join in the effort. Invite them to visit your church and see for themselves. People rarely walk in the door. They need to be told what we do and they need to be invited.

What does being a Christian mean to you? What difference has it made in your life? Tell people. That is how you evangelize. If everyone in the church would do this, people would be drawn to Christ and hopefully some of them would be drawn to your church.

Imagine your life without Christ. What would you miss? What would change in your life? Would you want that sort of change? I really doubt that you would.

The Rev. Edyth Pruitt at Fairview Presbyterian in Lenoir, NC gave a sermon some years ago in which she likened evangelism to an encore. You go to a concert and hear a magnificent performance. The audience goes wild as the concert ends, cheering and clapping. Everyone is on their feet shouting "Encore! Encore!" The performer returns to the stage and does another number. Often the audience calls for another encore or two.

The problem we have is that Jesus' phenomenal performance which ended with the crucifixion, resurrection and ascension also demands encore after encore but he isn't able, at least not for now, to walk back out onto the stage. He needed others to do the encore for him and he needs us to do the same. His encore is through the people he taught and who have been taught since then. The encore is up to you and to me and to every Christian out there.

I read a little book, <u>I've Just Seen Jesus</u> by Sandi Patty and Larnelle Harris. [1] This small book is full of conversion stories. One of these stories was titled "Mother Clarke and Jimmy the Rat". It was about a woman named Sarah Clarke and a drug addict identified only as Jimmy the Rat.

Mrs. Clarke operated a mission for the homeless and social outcasts in Chicago. Jimmy the Rat was addicted to various drugs and was homeless. He lived along with other homeless addicts on the streets, in the sewers and at times in a boarded up dark basement near Mrs. Clarke's mission.

On a Sunday afternoon he heard singing coming from the mission as they worshipped. He was listening to the singing when he was grabbed by someone, severely beaten, and left for dead. He was tossed out into the rain.

Somehow Jimmy survived and staggered to the mission, interrupting a worship service and asking for someone to pray for him.

Mrs. Clarke, Mother Clarke as she was called, and the mission workers went to Jimmy's aid and offered prayers for Jimmy the Rat. Jimmy found Jesus that day and accepted him as Lord and Savior. His life was permanently changed.

Jimmy had grown up on a farm in Indiana. He returned to that area and became a farmer himself. More importantly he became a spokesman for Christ. He married, raised a family, and became an outspoken evangelist using himself as an example that grace and salvation through Christ is available to anyone who accepts him as Lord and Savior, no matter what kind of life they had been leading previously.

Do you believe that some people are living in Hell on Earth? Jimmy the Rat certainly was. He was a down and out drug addict. His life was totally changed because Sarah Clarke reached out to him and he in turn became one of Christ's encore givers.

What might your motivations be for telling someone about Christ? Think about it, Pray about it. Most of us don't think about it or pray about it, but we should.

Jesus may come to some of us overtly as he did to Ananias when he told him to talk to Paul. He told me less overtly to go into the ministry but he did tell me. I kept resisting but finally did what I felt that he was telling me to do.

He is telling each of you also, perhaps more subtly than what he said to Ananias or to me but he is nevertheless telling each of you. You only have to listen and when you do, go out and talk to others.

If you truly want your church to thrive, that is what is required. Our churches have been doing God's work in incredible ways for hundreds of years but to continue that work requires that we all share our faith with others and bring them in to continue the great work of churches for hundreds of years in the future. We simply can't be happy and complacent, enjoying each other's company every week, worshiping together, and thinking that nothing will change in the future. It will change. There is no doubt

about that but how it will change depends upon our encore performances.
Amen.

1. Sandy Patti and Larnelle Harris, I've Just Seen Jesus, J. Countryman, division of Thomas Nelson, Inc., Nashville, TN, 2000.

Don't Pull the Weeds
Matthew 13:24-30, 36-43

Our gospel reading is a parable which only appears in the Book of Matthew, not in any of the other gospels. Most Bible translations call the story "The Parable of the Weeds". The King James Bible gives it the obscure title of "The Parable of the Wheat and the Tares."

This parable immediately follows the Parable of the Sower and follows the theme of that parable, an analogy between seed and people indicating that just as seed which is properly sown will grow and flourish, people of faith will similarly grow and flourish. The question raised is one which confronts any of us who grow anything, be it a lawn, a garden plot, or a vegetable farm. What should we do about weeds --- should we pull them, plow them under, or ignore them? The analogy is what should be done with people of no apparent faith or of weak faith. Should we try to get rid of them or expel them, drop them from the church roster --- plow them under so to speak?

With respect to gardening or farming, I once was of the pull-out-the-weeds school but gave that up years ago. When we moved into our current home, it was newly constructed and the lawn was Bermuda grass which I personally equate to a weed. It spreads everywhere even over paved roads and driveways, its roots dig in and cause damage to pavement, and it goes dormant and turns brown in the winter. So what did I do? I had the entire lawn sprayed with weed killer to eliminate the Bermuda grass, had the dead grass plowed under, and reseeded the lawn with fescue.

It looked great for a while until the Bermuda started to regrow from residual seed. The evil one was at work in my lawn but I was not about to be defeated. I had the lawn sprayed out again and reseeded once more with fescue. It looked great. No more Bermuda came up from residual seed and I was quite pleased.

But I forgot something --- my neighbors' lawns. They had Bermuda grass and, as I said, it spreads. It grows with long tendrils which spread out over an area and in time it spread from my neighbors' lawns into my lawn. It has not completely taken over and much of the fescue remains, but the Bermuda keeps spreading. I can control it by mowing the grass high, something the fescue likes and it shades the low growing Bermuda, keeping it under control. It is an uneasy truce between me and the two types of grass.

That kind of truce is what today's parable is about. To understand it you need to understand several things. First, the weeds Jesus is referring to in the parable are a specific kind of weed, "zizanion", a weedy rye grass which has poisonous seeds. It is also called "darnel". When it begins to grow, it looks like wheat. If it is pulled out, it is very likely that the wheat will be pulled out with it. It is also likely that wheat will be pulled out by people who think it is the darnel. It is extremely difficult to tell the two apart until the plants mature. Then they can easily be distinguished from each other. The darnel, the undesired poisonous weeds can be pulled out and burned, and the remaining wheat can be safely harvested. You just have to wait until you can easily distinguish between the two plants.

I can easily distinguish between Bermuda grass and fescue at all stages of their growth but if I try to pull the Bermuda grass, the fescue will come out with it so, for me, it is a losing battle --- a Catch 22.

Similarly, for humans, trying to weed out people of no apparent faith or of weak faith from our midst is a losing battle --- also a Catch 22. How would we ever be able to do that? We can't, and it is not our job in any event --- it is Christ's job. It is a message of grace.

Someone may appear on the surface to be very good and to have great faith. He or she goes through all the motions, participates fully in church activities and comes to worship every Sunday and yet, behind the scenes is a total hypocrite, always scheming to find ways of making personal gain through his or her church contacts. Just think of all of the politicians who have waved the flags of Christianity and of family values and later have been exposed as adulterers or thieves. They said or did something which exposed their true motives and they got caught in their duplicity. But many similar people will never be caught until the Day of Judgment.

On the other hand, some people may be very irregular participants in the activities of the church. They rarely if ever come to worship, except perhaps at Christmas and Easter. We see them on those rare occasions and may wonder if they shouldn't be confronted and asked to leave the church. After all, they aren't supporting the work of God --- or are they?

In truth, we don't know, but God knows. Do they have personal problems which prevent their regular participation? We don't know. Are they active in serving God through community and charitable activities? We don't know. We can't judge nor should we try.

The term "tares" instead of "weeds" in the King James Bible refers to something which is unwanted. The word is not used very much in today's English except in terms of weighing something. If you weigh something which is in a bucket or some kind of packaging or container, the weight that you measure will be false. It will include the weight of the container or the packaging. That weight is called the tare. You need to know the weight of the tare and deduct it from the total weight in order to have the true weight of the thing you are weighing.

An example which I am sure you are all familiar with is weighing yourself in the morning after your bath or shower. Then you get dressed and go for a doctor's appointment. When you step on the scale at the doctor's office, inevitably they come up with a weight which is five or more pounds higher. That added weight is your tare, the weight of your shoes, clothing and anything in your pockets. Your true weight is what they measured in the doctor's office minus your tare.

But what is the tare of a person's faith? You can't strip away the unseen agenda that the hypocrite has or the personal problems that the infrequent participant has to be able to determine their true tare and to assess how great their faith is. You can't and shouldn't try or jump to judgment. The doors of the church are open to all who wish to enter including hypocrites, those who are weak in faith, and sinners --- all of us. What we need to do is not to judge but instead to share with others what our faith means to us and to invite them to participate. Some of the most unlikely people you meet, people who you might at first blush tend to dismiss out of hand, could well be good seed. Do your best to plant them and to bring them to the good soil of Christ, the good soil that you have at your church.

As William Barclay [1] stated in his bible study <u>The Gospel of Matthew</u>:

"... the only person with the right to judge is God. It is God alone who can discern the good and the bad; it is God alone who sees all of a man and all of his life. It is God alone who can judge."

"So, then, ultimately this parable is two things --- it is a warning not to judge people at all, and it is a warning that in the end there comes the judgment of God."

Open your arms to people you meet. Tell them about your faith and invite them to share in that faith. Judgment is not necessary or desired. Accept them as they are. Invite them in. Invite them to share in the grace of our Lord, Jesus Christ. God will judge how worthy they are to receive that grace.

Alleluia. Amen.

1. William Barclay, The Gospel of Matthew, vol. 2, rev. ed., Westminster Press, Philadelphia, 1975

Living Water
Exodus 17:1-7; John 4:5-42

Since 1962 the National Aeronautics and Space Administration, NASA, has launched rockets to explore other planets. Two of these missions involved flying by Mars and ten have placed spacecraft in orbit around Mars. Six additional missions were designed to land on the red planet to explore it. Two more Mars landings are planned, one in 2018 and one in 2020.

These multi-billion-dollar space missions to explore Mars and other missions to the Moon and other planets, including spacecraft launched by Russia and China, are looking for minerals and mineable resources but most importantly are looking for water and possible life. Recently water has been found on Mars raising great excitement among scientists. Why? Why are they so concerned about finding water?

The answer is that water is life. Without it life as we know it cannot exist. Without water life as we know it would not be possible on other planets nor could humans go there and survive. Water is the most precious commodity in space and here on Earth. It is more precious than anything else. Without water we could not exist.

Many parts of the world, including the Near East, do not have an abundance of water. Good wells therefore are much in demand. Where the wells exist, towns grow around them, towns like Sychar in Samaria in Biblical times.

In the Bible, water becomes the focus of human concern time and time again. During the Exodus, the wanderings of the Israelites were much controlled by where they could find water. Moses had a near uprising on his hands when the people were without water at Horeb. God instructed him to strike a rock with his staff. He did so and water poured forth.

John the Baptizer baptized with water to symbolically wash away sin and baptism with water is one of the sacraments of our church. It is fundamental to being a Christian and symbolically connects us with the living water Jesus refers to in his conversation with the Samaritan woman at Jacob's well in Sychar. That living water is God. It is eternal life.

Jesus is thirsty and tired and goes to the well of Jacob for a drink where he encounters the Samaritan woman who is drawing water from the well with a bucket. He asks her for a drink and she responds in surprise. A Jew would never ask anything of a Samaritan, particularly not a Samaritan woman. Yet Jesus asks her.

It is noon, the heat of the day. Why did she come to the well then? It would have made more sense to come early in the morning when it was cooler. That is when the other women would have come but she came alone. Why? Possibly because she was an outcast herself she might have been avoiding other people intentionally. She may have been avoiding gossip about her and her five former husbands and about the man she was currently living with. She may have come at noon expecting solitude but she didn't get that. She encountered a Jew, Jesus, a Jew who spoke to her and who asked for a drink of water.

Max Lucado in his book Cast of Characters [1] commented that the Samaritan woman was streetwise. She thought that Jesus wanted something more than a drink. He could draw his own water if he wished. He must want something else, and indeed he did. He wanted her heart.

He also was respectful to her, something that she had not encountered from a man in a long time.

He told her of a different kind of water, water which would quench the thirst in her soul --- living water.

Think about this woman. She had five husbands and now was living with a man who was not her husband. She certainly would not have had a very good reputation in her community. In fairness to her, you need to remember that in that culture divorce was not the choice of a woman. Men could divorce their wives, not the other way around. A divorce was as simple as the man saying, "I divorce thee" and walking out. She couldn't do that. She was passed around from one man to another. Fred Craddock [2] said, *"She did not choose to take five husbands and another man. She was chosen; she had been passed around like a piece of meat. And now a new man says, 'Will you give me a drink?' Do you understand why she is defensive?"*

She is defensive and is astonished when this Jewish stranger tells her all about her life. He knows that she had five husbands. He knows that she is living with another man. But Jesus is a total stranger yet he knows all about her and talks to her about living water, water which will quench thirst forever.

Biblically, water is a symbol of Jesus, our living water. He met the Samaritan woman and asked her for a drink of water. Jesus said, *"Everyone who drinks this water will be thirsty again, but whoever drinks the water I give them will never thirst. Indeed, the water I give them will become in them a spring of water welling up to eternal life."*

The Samaritan woman encounters something new, something radical, in Jesus. He turns her whole life upside down. He ignores the social barriers of Jew-Samaritan and male-female and talks to her just as he might talk to anyone. He doesn't condemn her lifestyle. She hears about this mysterious living water and eternal life. She is totally changed.

She leaves her water jar at the well and hurries back into town telling people about her conversation with Jesus, telling them that he, a stranger, knows all about her, and asks if he could really be the long promised Messiah.

A crowd of Samaritans went with her back to the well. They went to receive that living water. They asked Jesus to stay with them. Jesus stayed for two days and many drank of the living water and believed in him. They said to the woman, *"We no longer believe just because of what you said: now we have heard for ourselves, and we know that this man really is the Savior of the world."* (NIV)

Whenever people go to Mars or the Moon or another planet, if they ever do, they may find the water they need to live. Two atoms of hydrogen and one atom of oxygen, H_2O, combine to form water. All life, plants, animals and humans, depends upon it. That is a fundamental fact on Earth, on the Moon, or on the planets.

One of the most successful international Christian charities is known as "Living Water." For more than 20 years they have been drilling boreholes to bring clean water to villages through the love of Christ in 23 countries. That is all they do --- drill boreholes and find water. As of early December 2013 they had drilled 12,797 boreholes literally providing life-giving water to hundreds of thousands of people.

They go deep into arid land to find water; just as future explorers of Mars may also have to do. Water is life. We can't live without it nor can we live eternally without the living water we receive from Christ Jesus.

Amen.

1. Max Lucado, Cast of Characters, Thomas Nelson, Nashville, TN, 2008
2. Fred B. Craddock, The Cherry Log Sermons, Westminster John Knox Press, Louisville, 2001

The First Will Be Last, and the Last Will Be First
Mark 10:17-31

When I wrote the title of this sermon on paper, I chuckled because it suddenly reminded me of something I did every few years when I was a Scoutmaster. If the Scouts were preparing their meal jointly, rather than individually when we were camping, when it came time to serve the food I would tell the boys to get their plates and to line up to be served.

Inevitably the bigger boys would push to the front of the line leaving the younger boys at the rear. Before anyone was served, grace would be said after which I would say, "About face" thereby reversing the order that the boys were in line and we would start serving the boys in the reverse order of how they originally lined up. The first would be last and the last would be first.

Those who were the smallest would receive their dinner before the bigger boys. The bigger boys had to give up their place in line and, if food began to run short, they might receive smaller portions than what they expected. No one would be left out at the end but some would end up with less than they had hoped for.

In a way, that is the message in our scripture reading today. This reading from Mark 10 is very familiar to you I suspect. The rich man asks Jesus what he needs to do to inherit eternal life and Christ's response stuns him. He walks away grieving. Jesus has told him to sell everything he owned and to give it to the poor --- in other words to get to the end of the line. He can't do it. His material possessions apparently mean more to him than salvation.

To fully understand our Gospel reading, let us look at it in three parts.

The reading begins with the rich man calling Jesus a *"Good teacher"* and Jesus responds with *"Why do you call me good? No one is good --- except God alone."* (NIV).

This response is sharp and was probably influenced by the culture of the times. In that culture, compliments often were used to conceal envy.

The rich man may have been implying that while Jesus was a good teacher, he was envious of Jesus' reputation and felt that he should have as great a reputation as Jesus does.

The next part of the reading is Jesus' instruction to the rich man to sell his possessions and give the money to the poor. Then he could follow Jesus.

In the culture of the times, this would have been forbidden. The rabbis forbad giving away all of one's property. They limited giving to 20 percent to prevent someone from being reduced to poverty. The rich man was told to ignore this and to give everything he had.

It is important to understand the culture of the times again. Back then, the average peasant would assume that anyone who was rich became rich by defrauding others, by taking more than his fair share. Tax collectors, for example, were well known for doing this. It was like the bigger Scouts getting into line first and serving themselves large portions at the expense of the smaller Scouts at the back of the line.

Throughout the New Testament the rich are condemned time and time again. In James 2:6 they oppress the poor; in Mark 12:40 and Luke 20:47 they take from helpless widows, and in James 5:1-6 they defraud their workers. There are many more examples.

Those who are "rich" in the New Testament are understood to mean those who are greedy and dishonorable unless they are acting in notably charitable ways. Thus, when Jesus told the man to sell his possessions, Jesus was asking the man to simply be returning to the poor what rightly was theirs to start with.

In the Old Testament, making restitution for a wrong normally meant adding one-fifth or 20% to the value of the goods lost. Restitution for theft of animals was much greater.

Later, in Judaism, this was changed and restitution required only a payment equal to the loss --- no penalty. But note the tax collector Zacchaeus in Luke 19:8 who realizes that his wealth was obtained by theft and offers fourfold restitution.

The final part of the reading is the absurd statement that a camel can go through the eye of a needle more easily that a rich man can enter the kingdom God. Jesus is deliberately being absurd.

The eye of a needle is very small and camels were the largest animals in Palestine. What Jesus is doing is rejecting any idea that one who is prosperous has received divine blessing. He makes it very clear that salvation is a divine decision and that wealth is not the only obstacle to salvation. *"Who can be saved?"* the disciples ask. Jesus responds that with man, salvation is impossible but with God all things are possible --- even salvation of a rich man.

As an aside, it has been thought by many that the "eye of the needle" or the "Needle's Eye" was the name of a gate in Jerusalem. This theory seems to have come from Theophylact in the eleventh century, more than a thousand years after the time of Christ. According to Clinton Arnold, there is no basis for that tradition. Jerusalem, as did other walled cities, had various gates. Large gates to allow passage of wagons, carts and animals often had a small built in gate or a small gate beside the large gate. The small gates were to allow people on foot to enter or leave the city when the large gates were closed. In some cases, it might have been possible for a large animal to squeeze through a small gate. Luke and Mark use different Greek words for "needle." If indeed the term referred to an actual gate, only one term would have been used. The conclusion then is clearly that Jesus was making the absurd reference to an actual needle's eye, not to a small gate with a tight fit for a camel.

William Barclay [1] says that Jesus, in this passage, "... *is turning accepted Jewish standards completely upside down. Popular Jewish morality was simple. It believed that prosperity was the sign of a good man. If a man was rich, God must have honored and blessed him. Wealth was proof of excellence of character and favor with God.*"

The disciples were surprised and would have argued that the more prosperous a man was, the better were his chances for salvation.

Jesus saw the dangers of prosperity and material wealth. The more one has, the more difficult it is to think beyond that or to consider giving it all away. To the contrary, the wealthier one is, the more likely he is to seek even greater wealth. A good example of this is the ever increasing salaries and bonuses of corporate executives even in poor economic times when employees are being laid off and profits for the company are declining. Possessions and money hold people's thoughts to this world, not to God's world.

The rich man did not understand this, and he didn't hang around long enough. Had he stayed, he would have heard that he could receive salvation in due course but not ahead of others. His wealth was meaningless so he should give it to those in need. Do God's work here on earth and you don't have to worry about salvation. By accepting Christ, you are assured of that, but you can't push ahead in the line. Jesus told the rich man to sell his possessions and follow him. He just walked away. He missed the greatest gift that God can give to anyone. **Amen.**

1. William Barclay, <u>The Gospel of Mark</u>, rev. ed., Westminster John Knox Press. Louisville, 1975

Applying for a Job Following Jesus
Mark 10:17-31, 46-52

In the preceding sermon I talked about the rich man who sought salvation from Jesus. This message is about a blind man with faith who seeks to have his sight restored. Both men are applying to Jesus for salvation, but only one of them gets what he seeks.

Jesus' reactions to the two men can be likened to a potential employer and how that employer reacts to applicants for a job. The way the employer is approached and the attitude of the applicant generally determines if the applicant will get the job or not, all things being equal. If two applicants are equally qualified, the choice generally falls to the attitude of each of the applicants and the impression they make on the employer.

I well remember my first job interviews when I was about to graduate from college. I wanted a job near to a university where I could pursue a Master's degree in night school.

I was invited for second interviews at a company in rural Tennessee and a company in Pittsburgh. I had prior campus interviews with these two companies and now I was invited by both of them for a second interview at their plants. It looked as though both were seriously considering me.

Now, there weren't many opportunities for graduate study in engineering in rural Tennessee back then, but there were numerous engineering graduate schools in Pittsburgh and in the other cities where that company had branches.

I declined the Tennessee Company and went for the interview with the Pittsburgh Company, United States Steel Corporation. The interview was at their corporate research facility. I put on my best suit --- my only suit in fact --- and went for the interview as nervous as a cat. I really wanted that job. I did my best to impress the people that I talked to and I thought things were going well.

I was taken to the company cafeteria for lunch. The entrée that day was spaghetti and on my way to the table with my tray, I stumbled and dumped a full plate of spaghetti all over the front of my suit. I was a mess, and I was sure that my chance for that job was out the window.

The people I was sitting with were very nice about it and

got me some napkins to wipe off the mess as much as possible. I got a fresh tray and the group I was with, several department heads, sat down.

Suddenly there was a bit of noise and I looked over to see a man face down in a plate of spaghetti. That man was one of US Steel's Vice Presidents. He suffered from narcolepsy, a sleep disorder which can cause someone to fall asleep without warning, which he did. He fell asleep and fell face forward right into his plate of spaghetti.

People ran to his aid and helped him to clean up a bit. I was a mess but he was worse. He had spaghetti on his face, his shirt and tie, and his suit.

The upshot of this was that after seeing what happened to this man, my nervousness completely disappeared. I spent the rest of the day interviewing with other company officials and left with the feeling that perhaps I still had some hope of getting hired. After all, if what happened to me could also happen to a company Vice President, maybe they would overlook my clumsiness or just take pity on me.

Well, whichever it was, I did get a job offer to work at their Chicago research facility. Chicago, of course, has several top universities. I accepted their offer and that started my career as an engineer and my entry into graduate school at the Illinois Institute of Technology.

Now, let us consider the differences between the rich man and the blind man, Bartimaeus. Both applied to Jesus for what they wanted. One was successful and one was not.

To remind you about the story of the rich man, consider that passage from Mark, but this time using Eugene Peterson's wonderful Bible paraphrase, The Message [1]:

"Good teacher, what must I do to get eternal life?"

"Why are you calling me good? No one is good, only God. You know the commandments ... "

"Teacher, I have from my youth kept them all!"

"Jesus looked him in the eye --- and loved him! He said, 'There's one thing left. Go sell whatever you own and give it to the poor. All your wealth will then be heavenly wealth. And come follow me.'"

"The man's face clouded over. This was the last thing he expected to hear, and he walked off with a heavy heart. He was holding tight to a lot of things, and not about to let go."

Today's scripture reading from Mark is paraphrased by

Peterson, in part, thusly:

"*As Jesus was leaving town ... a blind beggar by the name of Bartimaeus ... began to cry out, 'Son of David, Jesus! Mercy, have mercy on me!' Many tried to hush him up, but he yelled all the louder, 'Son of David! Mercy, have mercy on me!' ... Jesus said, 'What can I do for you?'*"

"*Rabbi, I want to see.*"

"*'On your way,' said Jesus. 'Your faith has saved and healed you.'*"

Both men approached Jesus with a request. The rich man wanted eternal life. The blind man had faith in Jesus and wanted his sight. Both of them, I am sure, wanted what they were asking for far more than I wanted that job. There are always other places to look for a job but there is only one place to go to seek eternal life and relief from lifelong blindness.

How do the two requests to Jesus differ and what is the difference between the rich man and the blind Bartimaeus?

First, it should be obvious to you that the rich man really wasn't rich. He was poor in faith and in his willingness to follow Jesus.

Bartimaeus, on the other hand, did not have sight, but he had vision. He could see and understand who Jesus was. He realized that Jesus was the Messiah as evidenced by calling him "*Son of David.*" He knew that Jesus could heal him if he wished.

How did the two men approach Jesus? The rich man was polite and respectful, just as a job seeker needs to be. The blind man wasn't. He interrupted Jesus and his followers. He kept shouting. He wasn't polite at all. Today that would kill his chances for a job if he approached a potential employer that way.

What did the two men say to Jesus and how did they say it? The rich man asked how he could get eternal life. He was concerned about himself, not others, and he was egotistical. He wasn't willing to give anything to others.

Bartimaeus had nothing and knew it. His words were simply, *"Jesus, Son of David, have mercy on me."* (NIV). He approached Jesus hat-in-hand. The rich man approached with bravado and self-importance.

The rich man tried to flatter Jesus. He wasn't open to hearing what Jesus said.

The blind man tossed off his cloak and came to Jesus. He gave himself away.

The rich man said, "From my youth I have kept the commandments." (NIV). He was proud of himself.

Bartimaeus said nothing except to request help. He was humble.

The young man seized the initiative and asked how he could obtain eternal life.

Jesus asked the blind man what he wanted. Bartimaeus didn't seize the initiative.

The results were that the rich man was told to sell what he owned, to give it to the poor, and then to follow Jesus. In other word, eternal life was there for him for the taking. All he had to do was accept the job offer to follow Jesus.

The blind man simply asked to be able to see. He already had faith.

You know the outcome. The rich man declined the job offer. He couldn't do what Jesus asked. His possessions meant too much to him. The blind man accepted the job offer – he received his sight and followed Jesus on the way.

On the face of things, if these two men were applying for a job today, the rich man probably would be hired. He was polite, respectful, and knew all the right answers. He probably would be a shoo-in.

Bartimaeus was crude, not polite, shouted out his demands, and produced no evidence that he had ever done anything right. He had spaghetti all over his cloak. He was a mess but he had faith.

He was "hired" as a follower of Jesus. He received his sight and eternal life.

The rich man wasn't "hired." The sad thing was that there were unlimited "job openings", and still are. It was in the rich man's power to be a follower of Jesus, to receive eternal life, but he missed that opportunity.

You know what it takes to get "hired" by Jesus. Have you done so? The fact that you are in church on Sunday morning says that you have, but don't rest on that assurance. Reach out and invite others to get "hired" by Christ.

Amen.

1.Eugene H. Peterson, The Message: Numbered Edition, NavPress, Colorado Springs, CO, 2005. (Scripture taken from THE MESSAGE. Copyright © 1993, 1994, 1995, 1996, 2000, 2001, 2002. Used by permission of NavPress Publishing Group.)

Blind Ambition
Mark 10:35-45

Our scripture reading from Mark, I am sure, is very familiar to you. The same story appears in Matthew 20:20-28 with one major difference. In Mark, James and John ask to sit at the left and right hand of Jesus, to effectively be his senior advisors and confidants. An analogy today might be a couple of Presidential campaign workers asking to be selected as the Vice Presidential nominee and as the Secretary of State.

The difference in Matthew is that James and John didn't make the request. Their mother Salome did. William Barclay [1] surmises that *"Matthew must have felt that such a request was unworthy of an apostle, and, to save the reputation of James and John, he attributed it to the natural ambition of their mother."*

Mark was probably being honest and wanted to show the disciples as what they were, ordinary men, not *"...a company of saints."* Jesus was using ordinary sinful people to change the world.

In any event, whether it was James and John who made the request, or their mother on their behalf, the story shows how flawed they were. They were full of blind ambition. They wanted status above that of the other apostles. After all, they were the ones chosen by Jesus along with Peter and they were Christ's closest friends. Why shouldn't they get some sort of special recognition? They certainly were not humble.

Being humble can be hard to do. The story is told of Dr. Clarence Bass, Professor Emeritus at Bethel Theological Seminary when, early in his preaching ministry, he gave a sermon in a Los Angeles church. He thought that it went quite well.

As he was standing at the door greeting everybody as they left the sanctuary, the remarks about his preaching were very complimentary, that is until a little old man commented, "You preached too long."

Dr. Bass wasn't fazed by the remark, especially in light of the many positive comments he had received. But then the little old man came through the line again, "You didn't preach loud enough" came another negative comment.

Dr. Bass thought it was strange that the man had come through the line twice but when the same man came through the third time and exclaimed, "You used too many big words" Dr. Bass needed some kind of explanation.

He sought out a deacon who stood nearby and asked, "You see that little old man over there --- who is he?"

"Aw, don't pay attention to him," the deacon replied. "He just repeats everything that everybody else says."

Never get too impressed with your own success or self-importance. Others many think otherwise about you. That is a lesson James and John had to learn.

The story is told in Mark and Matthew right after Jesus had once again predicted his death. Jesus has scarcely finished speaking when the brothers Zebedee asked for places of honor in the messianic kingdom. They wanted to be, and thought that they deserved to be, Jesus' chief ministers of state.

Dawn Wilhelm, in her book <u>Preaching Mark</u> [2], says:

"Their request is both outrageously selfish and utterly human. The sons of Zebedee ask that Jesus 'do for us whatever we ask of you.' In response Jesus asks ... 'What do you want me to do for you?'...They only know what they want, and they do not want to lead Vacation Bible School or clean dishes at the next potluck. They seek privilege, recognition, power, and glory when Jesus is enthroned." Their ambition is totally blinding them to what Jesus has been teaching them.

Their request shows, *"...as nothing else could, how little they understood what Jesus ... (had been) saying to them. Words were powerless to rid them of the idea of a Messiah of earthly power and glory."* It took a crucifixion to make them understand.

Jesus responds to their request by telling them that they have no idea of what they are asking. *"Are you able to drink the cup that I drink, or be baptized with the baptism that I am baptized with?"* (NIV). They say that they are able but they still don't understand.

We think of the cup and baptism as two sacraments but for James and John, at that point in time, they didn't. They probably thought that the cup referred to the cup of God's blessing in the 23rd Psalm, *"my cup overflows."* The reality was that it referred to a cup of bitterness and suffering, a cup which Jesus would prefer to forgo but which he accepts as being necessary to fulfill God's will --- the cup Jesus refers to later in the Garden of Gethsemane, *"Father, everything is possible for you. Take this cup from me. Yet not what I will, but what you will."* (Mark 14:36 – NIV)

According to Dawn Wilhelm, *"The water of baptism is also a dangerous image to those who suffer God's wrath. It recalls the harsh beginning of Jesus' ministry and anticipates his death and the death of others who will suffer the baptism of blood when they give their lives for the sake of the gospel."* The sacraments *"... of communion and baptism are associated with Christ's suffering, death, and resurrection."*

The ambitious, but naïve, Zebedee brothers announce that they are able, they can drink of the cup of Jesus and can be baptized as he is baptized. Yet, only days later they fall asleep in the Garden of Gethsemane and desert him when he is arrested.

Jesus knows what they will do --- how they will act --- but promises them that they will share in his cup and his baptism but not in the way they expect.

Jesus also tells them that it is not his to grant their request but that these places of honor are reserved for whom they have been prepared.

James and John angered the other disciples with their request and Jesus tells them that true greatness resides not in leadership or prominence but in becoming a slave, a servant, to all.

Jesus reminds the disciples of the gentile rulers, the Romans and their lackeys, who show their power with physical force, political intimidation, and patronage which seeks unquestioned loyalty.

Jesus expects an entirely different kind of leadership, one of servitude. He says, *"Whoever wants to be first must be slave of all."* (NIV)

William Barclay [1] commented that *"The basic trouble in the human situation is that men wish to do as little as possible and to get as much as possible. It is only when they are filled with the desire to put more into life than they take out, that life for themselves and others will be happy and prosperous."*

A poem of Rudyard Kipling titled "Mary's Son" expresses this spirit:

> *"If you stop to find out what your wages will be*
> *And how they will clothe and feed you,*
> *Willie, my son, don't go on the Sea,*
> *for the Sea will never need you.*
> *"If you ask for the reason of every command,*
> *And argue with the people about you,*
> *Willie, my son, don't you go on Land,*
> *For the Land will do better without you.*
> *"If you stop to consider the work you've done*
> *And to boast what your labor is worth, dear,*

Angels may come for you, Willie, my son,
But you'll never be wanted on earth dear!

The world needs those whose ideal is service --- not power. The world needs people who realize the sense of Jesus' words.

Jesus was the ultimate example. He is the Son of God. He could have had any kind of life he wanted --- a life of comfort, power, and authority.

Instead he gave all he had in service to others. He gave his life as *"a ransom for many."* Through his death and resurrection, through his suffering, he ransomed all of us from the sinful lives we live and assured us of salvation.

So what do you want? Do you want power and prestige or are you living a servant life?

Every four years we go to the polls to choose a President and numerous other officials to handle the affairs of government ---- local, state and national. By far, the great majority of candidates are servant people. They are willing and able to provide the kind of service that Christ was asking the disciples to provide.

But, as is always the case, some candidates may be seeking power and wealth more than they are seeking to serve. Analyze what they are saying, what they are doing, and what they propose to do before you make your choices. Do they have service to the people as their primary focus or do they have blind ambition? Make that analysis and then vote for those who you feel will act as Jesus expected his disciples to act.

I am sure that many of you act as Jesus would expect. You give countless hours in service to the church and community rather than seeking power and prestige. Those of you who are doing that are following Christ's pathway and I am sure are much happier for doing it than any amount of power and prestige would make you.

More often than not, I end church services with the words, "Go in peace. Serve the Lord." Do that, forget ambition, and your life will be much happier than it otherwise would be and you will be pleasing in the sight of God.

Amen.

1. William Barclay, The Gospel of Mark, rev. ed., Westminster John Knox Press. Louisville, 1975
2. Dawn Ottoni Wilhelm, Preaching the Gospel of Mark, Westminster John Knox Press. Louisville, 2008

The Heavens Declare the Glory of God
Psalm 19

On most Sundays, my sermons are based on one or more passages of scripture, typically an Old Testament reading, an epistle reading and/or a gospel reading. These readings for each Sunday are prescribed in the *Revised Common Lectionary*. It is used by most Christian churches and, over a three-year period, covers most of the Bible, and then the cycle starts anew. There is also a *Daily Lectionary* with readings for each day of the year. Thus, by following the Lectionary, particularly if you read it daily as I do, in a three-year period you effectively read a major portion of the Bible. So, by reading the Lectionary verses regularly one is constantly reeducating oneself about the scriptures and also about other writings which supplement them.

In addition to the Old Testament, epistle and gospel readings, the *Lectionary* also includes readings from Psalms, often multiple readings in the *Daily Lectionary*.

In services at many churches, more for want of time than anything else, Psalms are often not read although they frequently are included in many of the hymns which we sing and often in the Call to Worship, Call to Confession, and the Prayer of Confession. The Psalms are beautiful and poetic but, unlike the other readings are not as amenable to being used as the basis of a sermon. After all, they don't talk about Christ. They generally are poems of praise to God for what God has done or of lament for things that God has not done. It is a lot easier for a pastor to preach from the gospel or epistle readings which talk about Jesus than about a poetic reading from Psalms, and that is what we tend to do most of the time.

I am flying in the face of tradition and am using Psalm 19 as my text for this sermon, instead of the other Lectionary readings.

When I was preparing this message and when I read the Psalm, it triggered a memory of a short devotional service which I had conducted many years ago for a group of Scouts and of a sermon which I gave at another church based upon Psalm 19. Being a pack rat who rarely throws anything away, I dug through my files and found that other sermon and also found the old Boy

Scout devotional service. The idea for the Boy Scout devotional came from a November 1980 newspaper article that I had clipped and saved. I still have that original 1980 article which proves how much of a pack rat I am.

When I read that old devotional and reviewed the prior sermon, I immediately concluded that Psalm 19 would make a good basis for this message. Our scripture passage says that *"The heavens declare the glory of God; and the skies proclaim the work of his hands"*. (NIV). Go out at night on a cloudless night and look up at the skies. Look at the moon and stars, the constellations, the galaxies, the Milky Way and you can't help but be awed by the magnificence of God's creation. We don't see that in daylight. We have to look up at night. Psalm 19 goes on to say *"Day after day they pour forth speech, and night after night they reveal knowledge. They have no speech; they use no words; no sound is heard from them. Yet their voice goes out into all the earth, and their words to the end of the world."* We see much of God's creation during the day but what we see is limited to this tiny planet upon which we live and to the sun. At night, night does indeed declare knowledge. We realize, even without hearing words, the immensity of God's creation. Words are not needed, only our eyes to look up, to admire, and to wonder. It is very understandable why primitive cultures imagined that there had to be a multitude of gods to create something so magnificent.

That short devotional service was a long time ago, more than 20 years ago in February 1994. It was prompted by the fact that the March 1994 program theme for Boy Scouts was "Space Exploration" and I was using the devotional service to hopefully impress upon the Scouts that there is a lot more to exploring the heavens than rockets or satellites, but that those creations of humankind could give us greater insight into the handiwork of God.

Seldom is that handiwork been seen in greater glory than when a U.S. spacecraft or satellite flashed back spectacular close-ups from space. When photos of Mars, Saturn, Jupiter or even of Earth itself came into our living rooms or when the Hubble telescope sends back detailed pictures of far distant galaxies, we are awed by God's creations. To describe these celestial shows as spectacular is to understate reality. Even astronomers have been so awed by it all that they have had trouble finding an adequate description.

Yet the planets or the galaxies are but a tiny part of the

many billions of objects in the firmament, a space so vast that even our most sophisticated instruments have yet to probe its outer limits, if indeed there are any limits to the universe.

My wife Betsy and I have toured the Green Bank National Observatory in West Virginia and saw their huge telescope called the Robert C. Byrd Green Bank Telescope or GBT for short. This device is mammoth. It is literally as large as two football fields and yet can be turned in any direction and focus on distant objects in space with an accuracy of a few thousands on an inch, less than the thickness of a human hair. It is used to look far out into space at galaxies and objects far further away then was ever before possible, yet it can't see, or even begin to see, how large the universe actually is. This telescope is a radio telescope which intercepts radio waves given off by objects in space. The Hubble telescope, by contrast is an optical telescope which actually takes photographs of intergalactic objects.

We also get photographs from spacecraft which we launch to explore our own solar system. Some of the first such pictures of Saturn were beamed to us by the Voyager spacecraft from a point in the heavens so far away it would take *12 centuries* to get there on one of our modern Interstate highways. To reach the galaxies would take thousands of centuries. The GBT is looking much further into space than even that, and yet there appears to be no limit to the immensity of space.

I remember when the United States succeeded in launching its first satellite into orbit back in 1958. Dr. Werner von Braun, who had captained the team that turned the trick after another group failed, was beaming with satisfaction as he fielded questions from a huge corps of newsmen. By and by, a reporter asked him, *"Now that the Russians have two satellites in orbit and we have one, is there any danger of a collision up there?"* "Oh, I don't think so," said Dr. Von Braun, with that deadpan expression he used to spring on reporters now and then, *"After all, space is bigger even ... (than) Texas."*

And so it is. Indeed, the universe is not only bigger than Texas but it is so intricately intertwined that it mesmerizes the mind. *"One cannot be exposed to the law and order of the universe,"* Dr. Von Braun once wrote, *"without concluding that there must be a design and purpose behind it all."* To believe otherwise, to conclude *"that everything in the universe happened by chance,"* was in Dr. Von Braun's words, to *"violate the very objectivity of science itself."* For, he said, *"The better we understand the intricacies of the universe and all it harbors, the more reason we have to marvel at the inherent design upon which it is based."*

Dr. Von Braun acknowledged that *"Many men who are intelligent and of good faith say they cannot visualize a Designer."* But he added: *"Can a physicist visualize an electron? The electron is materially inconceivable and yet it is so perfectly known through its effects that we use it to guide our airliners through the night and take the most accurate measurements."*

"What strange rationale makes some physicists accept the inconceivable electron as real while refusing to accept the reality of a Designer on the grounds that they cannot conceive of Him?"

"After all," he said, *"must we light a candle to see the sun?"*

Former North Carolina Governor Jim Martin, in an article in the *Charlotte Observer* was quoted as saying, *"Science helps us to understand how God did it."* He was referring to how God created the universe and all creatures, including humans, who inhabit the earth, and quite possibly other planets out there in the vast firmament of space.

Dr. Warren Weaver, a noted mathematician said, *"...every new discovery of science is a further revelation of the order that God has built into His universe. God was the great mysterious mind that has created the infinite detail and the vast dimensions of the universe, including the crowning mysteries of you and me and our minds."*

"In church we sing 'Glory to God in the highest.' We need have no reservation about these words."

"With full credit to the science that has opened up the vastness of space and the universe beyond, God is still the highest."

When Christians celebrate the Lord's Supper we are celebrating that Jesus is our Lord and Savior. He is the God who created this magnificent universe and who came to us in human form and to be crucified that we might receive salvation. Pray for peace and peacemaking. Rejoice and be thankful for all of God's creation, for all that God has given us and for the salvation brought to us by Jesus, the Christ.

Amen!

(Based in part upon an article by John Troan, editor, in *The Pittsburgh Press*, November 23, 1980)

Poor in the World, Rich in Faith
James 2:1-17

There is a lot to consider in our scripture passage from James, part of which has in the past caused dissension in the church. Depending upon how you read this passage and other parts of the Book of James, you might conclude that salvation is by works, not by grace, which of course contradicts what we believe.

The contrast is so great that my resident consultant, Betsy, reminded me that Martin Luther was so incensed by the Book of James and this apparent contradiction that he wanted the Book to be excluded from the Bible.

Is there really a fundamental contradiction here? I don't think so, not at all. To me James is simply stating, or restating, the second of the two great commandments given to us by Jesus, *"Love your neighbor as yourself."* A Christian is expected to do that. It is a part of our job description if you will. Once we accept Christ as our Lord and Savior, assuming that we are sincere in that acceptance, we are saved by grace. That is a given.

But what does it mean to accept Jesus as our Lord and Savior? Doesn't it mean that we will follow his teachings? Doesn't it mean that we will love the Lord our God with all our heart, soul and mind and will love our neighbors as ourselves?

Can we truly love our neighbor by showing partiality? Can we love our neighbor by kowtowing to the wealthy one and ignoring the needs of the poor one? If we do that, are we truly showing love for all of our neighbors? I think not!

Fred Craddock, in one of his sermons, talked about two sixteen-year-old girls that he had seen in a short period of time. One girl wore a beautiful dress and as she came gracefully down a spiral staircase she was applauded by a waiting group of family and friends. She was a girl with everything.

The other girl was standing on the porch of a mountain cabin in eastern Kentucky holding a baby. The father was long gone and she was alone. She looked upon the gray world without any hope.

Craddock asks what the difference was in those two pretty sixteen-year-old girls. He asks, *"God, did you notice the difference?"* God answers, *"I didn't notice any difference."* Then Craddock says, *"God's getting a little old, have you noticed that? Losing eyesight and a little senile. Anybody can see the difference except God."*

The point is that God doesn't see the difference in any of his children, nor should we. Yet we often treat people differently based upon their appearance. We show favoritism for one group of people over another.

God prohibits such favoritism. James clearly illustrates this in our scripture reading. The reading opens with deference being given to a rich man in the synagogue. He is given the best seat while a poor man is made to stand or sit on the floor. We have all seen that sort of thing happen at one time or another. It might have happened to you.

For example, you might have made a reservation at an upscale restaurant for a special occasion. When you made the reservation you explained that you are celebrating a very special occasion and that you want a good table at 7:00 PM. You are assured that the table will be waiting for you.

You arrive on time for your reservation just as a car pulls up to the door and a person of prominence gets out and enters the restaurant in front of you. He doesn't have a reservation at all yet he is immediately escorted to a table. You give your name and say that you have a reservation. You are told, "Your table isn't ready yet. Please take a seat in the lounge and we will call you when your table is ready. Thirty minutes later you are called and are given the table at the rear of the dining room right beside the door to the kitchen. There is a constant noisy parade of wait staff coming and going in and out of the kitchen carrying trays. You look across the room and see the prominent person who was given a table without a reservation. He has the best table in the house, quite possibly the one which had originally been reserved for you. You have clearly been a victim of favoritism.

On the other hand, at one time or another, you too might have been the offender and have shown favoritism for one person over another when there was no reason to do so. Have you ever ignored someone who was poorly dressed in favor of someone who was not? Have you ever walked past a needy person on the street even though she clearly needed help? Have you preferred talking to people who you know well instead of always enthusiastically welcoming anyone who you have met for the first time at a social gathering or in church? Most of us can't honestly answer "no" to these questions. We humans are sinful and in that sin we show favoritism for some people over others.

Our scripture passage stresses the sin of favoritism for the wealthy or the well-to-do over the poor. James talks about keeping the "Royal Law" found in scripture meaning the Ten Commandments and Christ's two primary commandments, loving God and loving your neighbor as yourself. When you show favoritism, in the words of James, *"...you sin and are convicted by the law as lawbreakers. For whoever keeps the whole law and yet stumbles at just one point is guilty of breaking all of it."* (NIV).

Preaching Through the Christian Year by Fred Craddock and others [1], in referring to our scripture reading, reminds us that favoritism of the rich in preference to the poor is contrary to the Beatitudes. Luke 6:20 expresses the first Beatitude as, *"Blessed are you who are poor, for yours is the kingdom of heaven."* And in Luke 6:24 we read, *"But woe to you who are rich for you have already received your comfort."* (NIV)

Why was it necessary for Christ to say these things in the Beatitudes? It was necessary because favoritism and discrimination were as rampant then as they are now.

In 1st Corinthians 11:17-22, Paul is clearly addressing such favoritism and discrimination in the early church. He condemns those who *"...humiliate those who have nothing"* --- the "haves" discriminating against the "have nots."

Our scripture reading from James really is making one major point. That is that Christians should not show favoritism --- **period!** We are all equal under God's eyes and we must treat each other in that way.

To drive home that point, James makes it very clear that this is not a trivial item. He emphasizes that breaking a single point of the "Royal Law", no matter how minor it may seem to be, renders one guilty of breaking the whole law.

This is reinforced in Jesus' words as expressed in Matthew 5:19, *"Anyone who breaks one of the least of these commandments and teaches others to do the same will be called least in the kingdom of heaven, but whoever practices and teaches these commands will be called great in the kingdom of heaven."* (NIV)

You may remember Peter's words in Acts 10:34-35, *"I now realize how true it is that God does not show favoritism but accepts men from every nation who fear him and who do what is right."* (NIV)

The last few verses of our scripture reading, verses 14-17, are the verses which lead to the concern I mentioned at the beginning of this message that James may be suggesting that salvation comes from works, not grace. Those verses are:

"What good is it, my brothers and sisters, if someone claims to have faith but has no deeds? Can such faith save them? Suppose a brother or sister is without clothes and daily food. If one of you says to them, 'Go in peace; keep warm and well fed,' but does nothing about their physical needs, what good is it? In the same way, faith by itself, if it is not accompanied by action, is dead." (NIV).

This is not, contrary to Martin Luther's judgment, a statement which proclaims salvation through works, not grace. Quite the contrary, it reinforces the concept of salvation by grace.

One who truly accepts Jesus as Lord and Savior is saved by grace. The fact is that by accepting Christ, one should endeavor to act as he taught us to act. If we do not do that, can we truly say that we have fully accepted Christ?

Amen.

Thousands More Commandments
Mark 7:1-8, 14-15, 21-23

The first five books of the Old Testament, the Torah, contains 613 commandments, not just the 10 we are all familiar with. These 613 commandments were just the start of the rigorous set of rules that observant Jews lived by in the time of Christ. In addition to the Mosaic Law as expressed in the Torah, or the Pentateuch as it is also known, there were thousands of picayune additional rules in what was known of as the Oral Torah.

About 500 years before the time of Christ, the Jewish legal experts, the scribes, were not content with the rules they already had. They wanted to clarify and expand the Mosaic Law, the 613 commandments, so they started issuing more rules. In time they issued thousands and thousands of rules which governed every possible aspect of Jewish life. These new rules were not written down until many centuries later. They became known as the Oral Law or the Oral Torah. They became the traditions of the elders.

If you have seen the play or the movie *Fiddler on the Roof* you will recall, I am sure, the song "Tradition" and Tevye singing about the Jewish traditions --- how people dressed, what they ate, and on and on. In the play, Tevye says that he doesn't know why they did things the way they did. It was tradition and that was enough reason.

In our scripture reading from Mark, the Pharisees and scribes are criticizing Jesus because they noticed some of the disciples eating without first washing their hands. The scripture also says that nothing from the market could be eaten without first being washed and also that cups, pitchers and kettles had to be washed. The Pharisees and scribes cite the *"tradition of the elders"* to justify their complaints and ask why the disciples *"eat with defiled hands."*

On the face of things, based on what we know today about the need for cleanliness, the complaints of the Pharisees and scribes might seem to be reasonable. Yet Jesus takes exception to them and calls them hypocrites. He accuses them of abandoning God's commandments in favor of holding to human tradition. What did Jesus mean?

While hand washing makes sense to us for hygienic

reasons, that was not the reason that the Pharisees and scribes insisted on hand washing, not at all. They weren't concerned about hygiene. They were concerned with ceremony. By the rules of the Oral Torah, *"before every meal, and between each of the courses, hands had to be washed, and they had to be washed in a certain way. The hands, to begin with, had to be free of any coating of sand or ... any such substance. The water for washing had to be kept in special stone jars, so that it ... was clean in the ceremonial sense and so that it might be certain that it had been used for no other purpose, and that nothing had fallen into it or had been mixed with it,"* according to William Barclay [1].

Barclay goes on to say that *"the hands were held with finger tips pointed upwards; water was poured over them and had to run at least down to the wrist; the minimum amount of water was one quarter of a log, which is equal to one and a half egg-shells full of water. While the hands were still wet each hand had to be cleansed with the fist of the other. ... The fist of one hand was rubbed into the palm and against the surface of the other."*

Think about that. The hands are wet, and rubbed together but the water is now unclean because it touched unclean hands. How did they handle that?

Next the hands were held with the finger tips pointed downward; more water was poured over them starting at the wrists so that the water ran off of the finger tips. Now the hands were clean.

Barclay states that to fail to wash hands in this way was *"to be unclean in the sight of God."* It had nothing to do with hygiene or good manners. Eating with unclean hands was believed to make one subject to attacks of a demon and failing to wash hands in exactly the manner prescribed made one *"liable to poverty and destruction."*

To the Pharisees and scribes, these rituals, ceremonies and regulations were the essence of service to God. Their ethical religion was covered under a mass of taboos and rules. I could go on to cite many more of these extra commandments and rules, such as how to wash a kettle, but I trust that you see the point.

The scribes and Pharisees saw that the disciples of Jesus did not observe the niceties of the traditions and the code of the Oral Law and they asked why. Jesus responded by quoting Isaiah 29:13 where Isaiah accused people of honoring God with their lips while their hearts were elsewhere. In effect, Jesus accused the scribes and Pharisees of hypocrisy and of substituting human ideas for the laws of God.

The Pharisees and scribes *"depended on listening to the clever arguments and debates, the fine-spun niceties, the ingenious interpretations of the legal experts"* not to listening to God. Barclay says that *"Cleverness never can be the basis of true religion. True religion can never be the product of man's mind. It must always come not from a man's ingenious discoveries, but from the simple listening to and accepting the voice of God."*

Should the disciples have washed their hands before eating? Because of what we know today. <u>Certainly</u>. But was good hygiene dependent upon hand washing in the manner prescribed by the Oral Torah? <u>Certainly not</u>. The scribes and Pharisees were substituting a morass of rules and traditions for true worship and obedience to God. They were putting on a show for public consumption --- to impress others --- not to honor God and Jesus saw right through them.

Barbara Brown Taylor [2] calls the Pharisees and scribes a bunch of *"nit-picking legalists who reject Jesus' teaching because he keeps breaking their rules. They are holier than thou hypocrites who would rather be right than redeemed. Scripture helps us with these stereotypes by calling them blind guides, white-washed tombs, snakes, a brood of vipers --- all because they refused to believe the good news that their rules and regulations were no longer necessary, and they could trade all that in on a whole-hearted relationship with Jesus ... the Christ."*

"Jesus knows the full potential of our hearts for good and evil. He just wishes we knew it too. Meanwhile, he volunteers himself to everyone who still needs a scapegoat. I will take the blame, he says, you can give it to me. Give me what you hate, what you fear, out there and in here. I am not afraid of getting dirty. Germs don't scare me. Now sit down at my table, whoever you are. Take. Eat. This is my body, given for you."

Amen.

1. William Barclay, <u>The Gospel of Mark</u>, rev. ed., Westminster John Knox Press. Louisville, 1975
2. Barbara Brown Taylor, <u>Bread of Angels</u>, Cowley Publications, Cambridge, MA, 1997. All rights reserved.

613 Commandments
Acts 10:1-16

Proof texting is the use of a few words out of context from scripture to support an argument or belief without regard to the actual meaning of the entire scriptural passage.

In the New Testament, various theological debates based upon proof texting of Paul's letters to the Corinthians and the Galatians have divided Christian churches time and time again.

Even more divisive are disagreements based upon interpretation of Jewish law as expressed in the Torah, the first five books of the Bible. The Torah contains not only the Ten Commandments we all agree with but 603 other commandments. Devout Jews like Peter would scrupulously endeavor to obey all 613 of these commandments.

Some of the commandments are positive, like the one to rest on the Sabbath day. The majority however are negative. 365 commandments are prohibitions. Things that were to be avoided.

Some made great sense such as the prohibition against eating meat from an animal without a cloven hoof. The purpose of this was for health. Animals without a cloven hoof often carried disease organisms. Pigs in particular can carry trichinosis, a worm which if not killed by proper cooking can cause severe medical problems in humans. Considering that in those days there was no assurance that meat would be properly cooked, the Jews' answer was to simply prohibit any meat which might present a problem. Many of the commandments existed for similar reasons, reasons which made sense back then but which would be meaningless today. In fact, except for Orthodox Jews who still strictly observe the dietary laws, many Jews today do not.

Other commandments made no sense at all, at least not today, and probably were in the law for religious discipline purposes, not for any health of other reasons. For example, eating fresh grapes or raisins was prohibited.

Other commandments were to promote social welfare. For example, farmers were to leave a part of their crops unharvested for the poor.

Every seven years, other commandments required farmers

to leave their land unplanted and for loans to be forgiven.

Still other commandments are almost laughable today. Tattoos were prohibited. Men could not cut their hair or shave. Loans could not require payment of interest. Meat could not be eaten if cooked with milk or dairy products. So much for a cheeseburger or a Big Mac.

There are numerous commandments about sexual practices --- more than 20 of them, some of which make sense in today's world and some of which are nonsensical. For example, a member of the clergy was prohibited from marrying a widow or a divorcee.

It would take me all day to list all of the many commandments and that is not my point this morning.

In Christ, people were freed from most of these strictures. Jesus gave us guidance in how we should live. Basically, he gave us only two commandments to live by, that is to love the Lord our God with all our heart, soul and mind and to love our neighbors as ourselves. Effectively Jesus told us to follow the Ten Commandments as they really are incorporated in his two specifically stated commandments. Each of the Ten Commandments fits into either loving God or loving others. Jesus loved everyone and welcomed everyone. He didn't exclude anyone from his love and he didn't profess obedience to that huge array of commandments in the Torah.

His disciples plucked grain from the fields on the Sabbath, a violation of the Torah. The Pharisees took exception to this and Jesus rebuked the Pharisees. Jesus ate with sinners and gentiles. He broke commandment after commandment except for the original Ten Commandments. Why then should we as Christians get hung up on those obscure 603 commandments in the Jewish law? Those commandments were from the covenant God gave to the Jews at the time of Moses. Christ gave us a New Covenant which replaced all of that yet, even today, Christians get hung up over those old laws which no longer apply. If some of us get hung up over these old laws, can you see the quandary Peter got into in our scripture reading this morning? He followed the old laws, for the most part, although he was slowly moving away from them.

In our scripture reading, it is stated that he was staying at the house of Simon the tanner, which in itself was a violation of Jewish law. A tanner worked with bodies of dead animals. Thus Simon was permanently unclean. For a Jew to accept hospitality from any unclean person was unheard of. According to William Barclay [1], *"It was his uncleanliness that made it necessary for Simon to dwell ... outside the city. No doubt this tanner was a Christian and Peter had begun to see that Christianity abolished these petty laws and taboos."*

Peter was staying with Simon the tanner when the servants of Cornelius were sent to fetch him. Cornelius was a Roman army officer, a gentile, who was a devout and God-fearing man. Note that the scripture refers to him as "God fearing". We are not sure but the term suggests that he may have been circumcised as that term applied to circumcised gentiles who worshipped God. Cornelius had a vision in which an angel told him to seek out Peter. Cornelius was willing to be instructed and guided by Peter and his vision directed him to Peter.

As Cornelius' servants were approaching, Peter was on the roof of the house praying when he too had a vision, a vision of a sheet being lowered containing all kinds of unclean animals, reptiles and birds (except seafood, which of course needed water not to die). A voice tells Peter to slaughter the animals, reptiles and birds and eat. Three times the voice commands Peter to do this but this is too much for Peter. Staying in the house of an unclean person is one thing, but breaking the dietary laws is another thing altogether.

William Willimon [2] commented that, only these laws stood in the way of the assimilation of gentiles into the church by the Jews. The laws *"... identified, demarcated faithfulness in the midst of incredible pressure to forsake the faith, drop one's particularities and become a good citizen of the (Roman) Empire. A little pork here, a pinch of incense to Caesar there, and it will not be long before the faith community will be politely obliterated. We must not read this story from the safe vantage point of a majority religion ... (but) ... from the minority point of view, people for whom a bit of pork or a pinch of incense or a little intermarriage was a matter of life and death for the community. The dietary laws ... are a matter of survival and identity for Jews. And yet, can it be that these laws are being supplanted by some other basis for survival and identity? No wonder Peter is left baffled."*

Peter was a Jew as were the other apostles. The twelve would think just as Peter did yet here Peter has a vision telling him to forget all of that. The old laws don't apply to Christians. The old taboos and prohibitions are gone. Much of what Peter had always observed was no longer applicable. He refuses to break the dietary laws and the voice tells him, *"Do not call anything impure that God has made clean."* (NIV). The sheet and animals disappear back to heaven.

Peter was on the roof of the house and about then would have stood at the railing around the roof and seen Cornelius' messengers approaching. Why would there have been a railing? Simply because one of the 613 commandments required a railing, a sensible thing for a flat roof. Not all of the laws were unreasonable. A railing makes sense for a flat roof where people often slept. The roofs also often had a sheet over them to shield people from the sun. Peter's vision may have been prompted by such a sheet. In any event, Peter greeted the messengers and that was the start of his acceptance of the first gentile Christian, Cornelius.

If we as Christians wait for others to come to our door and seek to become Christians, or if we wait for non-Christians to walk in the door of this church to join with us, few, if any, new people will come to Christ. Cornelius was the start for Peter and after that Peter reached out to gentiles. We need to reach out to others in as many ways as we can. We need to reach out to the poor, to minorities, to sinners no matter what their sins are, and offer them the grace and salvation of our Lord and Savior, Jesus Christ.

Amen.

1. William Barclay, The Acts of the Apostles, rev. ed., The Westminster Press, Philadelphia, 1976
2. William H. Willimon, Acts: Interpretation, A Bible Commentary for Teaching and Preaching, John Knox Press, Louisville, 1973

Pray for Everyone
1 Timothy 2:1-7

Who do you pray for? Most of us pray for our families, our friends and neighbors --- particularly those with medical or other problems, people in our community, and often for our political leaders, police, EMTs and firefighters, and our military.

We often pray for ourselves --- that an illness will be healed, that difficulties we encounter will work out, that financial problems will be solved, and more.

Those kinds of prayer are what we expect people to pray for and there is nothing wrong with that but in our scripture reading from 1 Timothy, Paul is telling us that our prayers need to be broader than that. He tells us to pray for everyone, without exception. Without exception? Yes, without exception!

What about dictators? Would you have prayed for Adolph Hitler or Muammar Gaddafi?

What about notorious criminals like Al Capone or Babyface Nelson?

What about terrorists and terrorist organizations like Al Qaeda and ISIS?

Yes, pray for all of them and all like them!

When Paul wrote his letter to Timothy, Nero was emperor of Rome and Paul said to *"...pray for kings and all those in authority."* In other words, pray for Nero, a monster who cruelly persecuted Christians.

Peter said, *"... fear God, honor the emperor."* (1 Peter 2:17).

Pray for Nero --- honor him! That would have been incredibly hard to do just as it would be for us to pray for Vladimir Putin or Kim Jong-un. In an election season we may be praying for our political party and our favored candidate. But also praying for the other political party and the other candidate would be very difficult to do. And what if you don't care for either of the Presidential candidates, could you pray for both of them?

Praying for everyone seems to be an oxymoron, doesn't it? Why should you pray for people you disagree with or people who are evil and corrupt?

The early church prayed for these kinds people and urged Christians to pray for their political leaders, as should we

It is fundamental that we pray for everyone, as hard as that may be at times. 1st Timothy says, *"This is good, and pleases God our Savior, who wants all people to be saved and to come to a knowledge of the truth."*

Leslie F. Brandt [1] has expressed Paul's epistles in poetic form with today's scripture reading as:

"God's commission to His children concerns the spiritual welfare of all men and women.

This means that God's will, our objective, is the salvation of the whole human family.

We should, of course, offer our prayers to God on behalf of, and extend our efforts to witness in word and deed to, every human being --- from our leaders and executives in high places to the laborer, the poor, the uneducated, and the oppressed.

There is only one God, and that is the God that Christ revealed.

This is the only God that we can worship and serve, and we are the ministers of this God to the people of our world.

Salvation does not come to us by way of the Law, but the accepting and propagating of God's love through Christ does impose upon us certain responsibilities."

The charge to pray for everyone goes against our grain with respect to certain individuals but it is what God wants us to do, as hard as that may be.

In a way, our scripture reading is telling us to act as the apostles did when they were fishermen. They cast a wide net to bring in as many fish as possible. Then Jesus told them to fish for people instead.

Our scripture reading is telling us to cast a wide net, a net of prayer for all humanity.

The prophet Ezekiel said, *"Do I take any pleasure in the death of the wicked? Declares the Sovereign Lord. Rather, am I not pleased when they turn from their ways and live?"* (Ezek. 18:23) and *"For I take no pleasure in the death of anyone ... Repent and live!"* (Ezek. 18:32). (NIV).

And in 2nd Peter 3:9 we read, *"The Lord is not slow in keeping his promise, as some understand slowness. Instead he is patient with you, not wanting anyone to perish, but everyone to come to repentance."* (NIV).

Pray for everyone, even those with whom you disagree, to accept Christ and for their salvation. That is the message of our scripture reading today or, putting it in another familiar way, pray without ceasing.

Amen.

1. Leslie F. Brandt, Epistles / Now, Concordia Publishing House, St. Louis, ©1974, 1976. Used by permission. All rights reserved.

Centering Your Life
Jeremiah 18:1-11; Luke 14:25-33

Have you ever tried to make something on a lathe or a potter's wheel? If so, you know how important it is to have your work centered.

Both the lathe and the potter's wheel require the wood or clay you are working with to be centered. Otherwise what you are trying to make will not be perfect --- quite the contrary --- it is likely to be a mess.

For the lathe, if the piece of wood is not centered, it wobbles and is hard to cut, at best resulting in a finished product with uneven grain and, at worst, resulting in a worthless piece of wood which is good for little more than kindling.

The potter's wheel is more forgiving than the lathe. With it a lump of clay must be centered on the wheel in order to create a perfect piece of pottery. If it is off-center, the piece will wobble and the result will be a malformed article. However, the clay is forgiving and can be mashed down, replaced on the center of the wheel, and reworked. The clay, unlike the wood on the lathe, is malleable and can easily be reworked.

You can't hide the fact that your work on the lathe or the potter's wheel was not centered to start with. The results speak for themselves.

Similarly, we can't hide our flaws from God. God knows if our lives are centered or not. He knows what our capabilities are and expects us to make the most of them. God is our potter and we are his clay. If we aren't centered on God, God cannot work with us. It is all too easy to center our lives on material things, on everyday activities, on friends and family, to the exclusion of God.

That is the message of our scripture readings from Jeremiah and from Luke.

The reading from Luke comes across as being harsh, very harsh. The <u>King James Bible</u>, the <u>NIV Bible</u>, the <u>New Revised Standard Bible</u> and some other Bible translations say that we must **hate** our father, our mother, and our other family members. Surely we are not being told to hate our family. Our God of love surely would not ask us to do that --- and he doesn't. In the context of the scripture reading we are really not being told to hate but instead are being told to center our lives on God, rather than on family.

The Living Bible [1] translates verse 26 of the reading from Luke as, *"Anyone who wants to be my follower must love me far more than he does his own father, mother, wife, children, brothers, or sisters --- yes, more than his own life --- otherwise he cannot be my disciple."*

That is a markedly different translation. It certainly doesn't tell us to hate our family. Rather it stresses that we must center our lives on Christ.

The Good News Bible translates verse 26 similarly.

Peterson's The Message [2] uses these words, *"Anyone who comes to me but refuses to let go of father, mother, spouse, children, brothers, sisters --- yes, even one's own self! --- can't be my disciple."*

This particular passage of scripture graphically illustrates the trap that we can get into by taking any part of scripture literally. The Bible is the inspired Word of God but it has been translated by fallible human beings and no translation is without error, nor are they infallible or inerrant.

Even though some Bible translations use the word "hate" in referring to family, *"Jesus is clearly not telling the crowd to hate their parents and abandon their children. He is sharply confronting them with the priority of their commitments and implicitly pointing them to the new surrogate family they join as disciples."* [3].

Our Lord and Savior showed his love for everyone and never taught us to hate anyone, most of all our family. What matters is to interpret scripture in context, not one line at a time.

The context here in our two scripture readings is centering --- centering our life on God --- not on other things or other persons.

Where is the center of your life --- material possessions, friends, family, or God? If you are not willing to place God at the center of your life you cannot be a successful Christian.

Are you pulled away from your commitment to God? Does the urgency of life pull you away from visiting the sick, from telling others about Christ, from tending to the needs of others, from prayer, from worship?

God is our potter. We are his clay. We must remain centered on him. If we will not do that, God cannot work with us. It is our responsibility --- ours alone!

Center your thinking on him and he will mold and shape you. Remain centered on God's vision, not on your own vision.

Amen.

1. <u>The Living Bible Paraphrased</u>, Tyndale House Publishers, Wheaton, IL, 1971
2. Eugene H. Peterson, <u>The Message</u>: Numbered Edition, NavPress, Colorado Springs, CO, 2005. (Scripture taken from THE MESSAGE. Copyright © 1993, 1994, 1995, 1996, 2000, 2001, 2002. Used by permission of NavPress Publishing Group.).
3. Charles B. Cousar, <u>Texts for Preaching - Year C</u>, Westminster John Knox Press, Louisville, 1994.

Do You Understand What You Pray for?
Matthew 6:5-15; Luke 11:1-13

Luke 11:1-13 and Matthew 6:5-15. both discuss Jesus telling the disciples and us how to pray and both readings include versions of the Lord's Prayer. We say the Lord's Prayer week after week but do we really pray that prayer or just recite it without really thinking about it? What does God think when he hears us say the Lord's Prayer? Let us imagine God listening to our prayer and responding to what we say:

Our Father who art in heaven
Yes?
Don't interrupt me. I'm praying.
But you called Me!
No, I didn't call you. I'm praying.
Our Father who art in heaven.
There --- you did it again!
Did what?
Called Me.
You said, "Our Father who art in heaven"
Well, here I am. What's on your mind?
But I didn't mean anything by it.
I was, you know, just saying my prayers for the day.
I always say the Lord's Prayer.
It makes me feel good, kind of like fulfilling my duty.
Well, all right. Go on.
Okay, hallowed be thy name.
Hold it right there.
What do you mean by that?
By what?
By "Hallowed be thy name"?
It means, it means ... good grief, I don't know what it means.
How in the world should I know? It's just a part of the prayer.
By the way, what does it mean?
It means honored, holy, wonderful.

Hey, that makes sense.

I never thought about what 'hallowed' meant before, thanks.

Thy kingdom come, Thy will be done, on earth as it is in Heaven.

Do you really mean that?

Sure, why not?

What are you doing about it?

Doing? I just think it would be kind of neat if you got control of everything down here like you have up there. We're kinda in a mess down here you know.

Yes, I know. But, have I got control of you?

Well, I go to church.

That isn't what I asked you.

What about your bad temper? You've really got a problem there, you know.

And then there's the way you spend your money --- all on yourself.

And what about the kind of books you read?

Now hold on just a minute! Stop picking on me!

I'm just as good as some of the rest of those people at church!

Excuse Me. I thought you were praying for my will to be done.

If that is to happen, it will have to start with the ones who are praying for it.

Like you --- for example.

Oh, all right. I guess I do have some hang-ups.

Now that you mention it, I could probably name some others.

So could I!

I haven't thought about it very much until now, but I really would like to cut out some of those things. I would like to, you know, be really free.

Good. Now were getting somewhere.

We'll work together --- you and Me. I'm proud of you.

Look Lord, if you don't mind, I need to finish up here.

This is taking a lot longer that it usually does.

Give us this day our daily bread.

You need to cut out the bread. You're overweight as it is.

Hey, what a minute! What is this? Here I was doing my religious duty, and all of a sudden you break in and remind me of all my hang-ups.

Praying is a dangerous thing. You might get what you ask for.

Remember, you called Me --- and here I am. It's too late to stop now.

Keep praying. (pause). Well, go on.

I'm scared to.

Scared? Of what?

I know what you'll say.

Try me.

Forgive us our sins as we forgive those who sin against us.

What about Mike?

See, I knew it! I knew you would bring him up!

Why, Lord, he's told lies about me, spread stories.

He never paid back the money he owes me.

I've sworn to get even with him!

But --- your prayer --- What about your prayer?

I didn't --- mean it.

Well, at least you're honest.

But, it's quite a load carrying around all that bitterness and resentment, isn't it?

Yes, but I'll feel better as soon as I get even with him.

Boy, have I got some plans for him.

He'll wish he had never been born.

No, you won't feel any better. You'll feel worse. Revenge isn't sweet.

You know how unhappy you are --- well, I can change that.

You can? How?

Forgive Mike. Then, I'll forgive you.

And the hate and the sin will be Mike's problem --- not yours.

You will have settled the problem as far as you are concerned.

Oh, you know, you're right. You always are.

And more than I want revenge, I want to be right with You. (sigh)

All right, all right ... I forgive him.

There now! Wonderful! How do you feel?

Hmmmm. Well, not bad. Not bad at all.

In fact, I feel pretty great!

You know, I don't think I'll go to bed uptight tonight.

I haven't been getting much rest, you know.

Yeah, I know.

But you're not through with your prayer, are you? Go on ...

Oh, all right.

And lead us not into temptation, but deliver us from evil.

Good! Good! I'll do that.

Just don't put yourself in a place where you can be tempted.

What do you mean by that?

You know what I mean.

Yeah. I know.

Okay. Go ahead ... finish your prayer.

For Thine is the kingdom,

and the power, and the glory forever. Amen.

Do you know what would bring me glory ---?

What would really make me happy?

No, but I'd like to know.

I want to please you now.

I've really made a mess of things.

I want to truly follow you.

I can see now how great that would be.

So tell me ... How do I make you happy?

You just did!

Amen.

Note: The author of the two-person prayer and response is unknown.

Will God Answer Your Prayers?
Luke 11:1-13

Our scripture reading from Luke is really two messages, not one. Jesus prayed often and his prayers were directed to his Father, God, and in the first four verses of Luke 11 he teaches the disciples, and us, how to pray. The prayer he teaches is the same prayer that we pray every Sunday, the Lord's Prayer.

Jesus was praying and the disciples, seeing him praying, asked him to teach them how to pray. He responded offering a prayer in three petitions, the first petition being to address God in an intimate manner as Abba, or Father in English, and to honor him. According to the Zondervan Commentary [1], *"hallowed be your name, your kingdom come"* points both to God's ultimate victory at the establishment of his kingdom and to hallowing his name through righteous living. Jews would never speak the name of God, hence the references to "you" and "your name". In synagogues then and now a prayer called the Qaddish is recited after the rabbi's sermon which addresses God in the same manner.

The second petition in the Lord's Prayer is for sustenance, "our daily bread" and the reference to "daily" harkens back to the manna the Israelites received each day in the desert during the Exodus.

The third petition is for forgiveness and avoidance of temptation. In this context, the word "temptation" can be misleading. God does not tempt us, but sin does, and that is what the prayer asks, that we will not be tempted by sin.

This then is how Jesus taught us to pray. We pray to our God in an intimate manner which honors him, we pray for the necessities of life, and we pray for avoidance of sin's temptations.

Note that we aren't taught to pray for our druthers, things we want but can do without. For most of my life I have wanted a Mercedes Benz 300SL gull wing roadster. I even have a scale model of one on my desk but somehow or another God has not seen fit to give one to me. I don't need it and certainly can't afford it but I want it. But praying for it will never work. We are only to pray for what we truly need and, unfortunately I don't need that Mercedes, and I don't think it is on God's priority list.

I do get a kick out of athletes and coaches who go into a

huddle before a sports event to pray for victory. That is not prayer, it is nonsense. Carolina prays for victory over Duke. Duke prays for victory over Carolina. And on and on. God isn't going to pay attention to such prayers. Among other things, they are selfish and self-serving. They certainly are not prayers for the necessities of life and they are not prayers to honor God.

The remaining nine verses of our scripture reading are a parable which addresses hospitality and asking for what you need, not what you want.

In the parable a traveler has arrived at a home seeking shelter at around midnight. In Biblical times people had an almost sacred duty to provide hospitality. The homeowner did not have food to provide to his guest, so he went and banged on his neighbor's door asking for bread.

Recognize that back then people left their door open all day and did not close it unless they were sleeping and wanted privacy. You simply didn't knock on a closed door unless it was an emergency. But not being able to show proper hospitality was an emergency in that culture.

Picture the neighbor's house. It would probably have had only a single room and one tiny window. The floor would have been packed dirt and part of the floor would have a raised platform with a charcoal stove which was kept burning all night for warmth. The family would have slept on mats around the stove and the mats would have been close together for warmth.

Any livestock --- chickens, goats, lambs, etc. --- would also be in the house at night.

For the neighbor to get up to answer the knock on the door would disturb the entire family, not to mention the livestock.

In the parable, the neighbor does eventually arise and provides what was requested, if for no other reason than that he would be shamed if he did not offer help regarding hospitality. In the community he would be talked about if he did not respond to the plea. It was far better to awaken the family and disturb the animals than to be reproached by the villagers if he refused the request.

The point of the parable is that if our friends answer our appeals, even if unwillingly, how much more will God respond to our appeals to him who desires to give us his kingdom.

Jesus is teaching the disciples and us how to pray and he *"... instructs us to ask for whatever we need, to knock expectantly, and to pray like someone banging on the door."* (These Days, March 7, 2016)

James Brashler [2] said, *"The message of the parable is that a shameless request in order to provide hospitality and responding to a neighbor's need even when it is inconvenient demonstrates the kind of shameless praying Jesus commends ...*

"If sinful human parents will give their children the good things they ask for rather than giving them dangerous things, Jesus continues, certainly God the Father will go far beyond the responses of human parents by giving the Holy Spirit."

But in your prayers, remember that God is the sole judge of what we truly need. He won't pay much attention to your druthers, to my Mercedes Benz 300SL, or to Carolina or Duke Basketball.

Amen.

1. Zondervan Illustrated Bible Backgrounds Commentary, Volume 1, Clinton E. Arnold, ed., Zondervan, Grand Rapids, MI, 2002.
2. James A. Brashler, in *Presbyterian Outlook*, Vol. 196, No. 26, Dec. 22, 2014.

Women's Lib in Judea
Luke 10:38-42

I am sure you are familiar with today's very short scripture reading from Luke, but what does it really mean?

Is the younger sister Mary just goofing off and letting her older sister Martha do all of the work? After all the house is full of guests with Jesus and his disciples and there is a lot of work to be done to prepare a meal for them, yet Mary is ignoring that and is just sitting there listening to what Jesus has to say. Is that fair? Shouldn't she be helping Martha?

Another take on the scripture, one you likely have heard before, is that it was far more important for Mary to be listening to the words of Jesus than to be concerned about helping to prepare the meal. I think that most of us would side with Mary on this issue. After all even Jesus said that Mary had made the correct choice. So that's it --- right? No, wrong!

The scripture reading is far more meaningful than Mary simply making the choice of listening to Jesus instead of helping Martha --- far, far more meaningful.

In a way it was women's lib in Judea, of all places, 2000 years ago.

Let us look at the scene and the culture of the times more closely. If there ever was a time and place in history where the phrase "a woman's place is in the home" was more culturally descriptive, it was probably in the highly patriarchal society of Biblical times.

According to Fred Craddock [1], in today's story Jesus is visiting a woman, Martha, who is "... *so busy serving that she does not hear the word, and Jesus offers her an example, her sister. To the man, Jesus said to go and do; to the woman, Jesus said to sit down, listen, and learn.*"

But there is more to the story than that. Martha is trying her best to be a good hostess. That is what the culture of the times expected. A woman should serve the guests and not be concerned with other things. But our women's libber, Mary, doesn't think that way. She sits at Jesus' feet to listen to him. She forgets about hospitality and opts to learn what she can. This was the better choice in Jesus' eyes, but it meant far more than that, far more than Mary shirking her duties and not doing any work.

There is a great symbolic lesson here.

First, in that culture it simply was not considered to be proper for men to visit the home of single women where a man was not present. It just wasn't done and scripture gives us no indication that there was anyone else at the home other than Mary and Martha. So Jesus was breaking tradition to even go there and Martha was breaking tradition by asking him in.

The tradition of the times was also that a rabbi, such as Jesus, would never waste any time sharing his wisdom with, **gasp, a female**. It just wasn't done but here was Jesus doing it.

Then there is the fact that our women's libber, Mary, sat at Jesus' feet. **Wow! What a scandal!** Only those who sat at the feet of a teacher were his disciples. Did this mean that Mary was a disciple? Did Jesus really have women disciples? Emphatically yes! Christ had far more than twelve disciples and many of his disciples were women. Rabbis never had women as disciples, but this one did. Christ, in a way, was the first leader of the women's liberation movement some 2000 years ago.

The shocking nature of Mary's action is emphasized by the fact that back then girls never received any kind of formal education. They were taught only household duties --- sewing, weaving, cooking, and the like.

The Mishnah, the first major work of rabbinic literature said, "… if a man gave his daughter a knowledge of the Law it is as though he taught her lechery." Women simply were excluded from any form of education, even via worship in the synagogue. Back then the synagogue was a male bastion. It was a men's club. No women were allowed. Even today, men and women generally sit separately at Jewish and Muslim services.

So, while Martha was playing her traditional role, Mary was breaking new ground and Jesus was breaking cultural traditions and expectations and was affirming the status of women as Christ's disciples. Mary was playing the role of a liberated Judean woman.

Amen.

1. Fred B. Craddock, <u>Interpretation: Luke</u>, John Knox Press, Louisville, 1990.

The Bay of Pigs
Galatians 3:23-29; Luke 8:26-39

I have to begin this message with a confession. I stole the title of today's sermon from one given by the Rev. Edyth Pruitt of the Fairview Presbyterian Church in Lenoir, NC. Why? I just liked it and it is very appropriate, particularly when considering the scripture reading from Luke about the man who was possessed by demons.

Both of our scripture readings are about acceptance, but in 180-degree opposite ways.

In Galatians we read, *"So in Christ Jesus you are all children of God ... There is neither slave nor free, nor is there male and female, for you are all one in Christ Jesus. If you belong to Christ, then you are Abraham's seed, and heirs according to the promise."* (NIV).

Jesus excludes no one, but many Christians do exclude others, often because of how they look, how they are dressed, how they act, where they came from, and so forth. We tend to be judgmental of others. We don't seem to trust those who are "different" ---those who are not like us.

Our scripture reading from Luke is an extreme example of a person not being accepted --- so much so that he was totally rejected by society. He was an outcast and was forced to live in a cemetery. He was demon possessed. He was mad and was rejected. In fact, he had been chained up multiple times but managed to break his chains and escape. He was naked and alone when Jesus found him.

How would you react if you saw a naked, dirty, angry man who lived in a cemetery? Most people would give him a wide berth and likely would call the police.

"9-11. What is your emergency?"

"There is a naked wild man living in the cemetery. Do something."

Well Jesus did something, something that angered the people. He exorcised the demons that possessed the man.

To understand this, you need to understand what it meant to be demon possessed in the first century. In that time, a demon was considered to be an unclean spirit or even a fallen angel. A demon was believed to be a spiritual entity, a malevolent force which could inhabit a person or animal. Demons were the work of Satan. They were feared and anyone who was believed to possess a demon was rejected by society.

Whenever anyone suffered from mental illness or epilepsy or just acted in a non-conventional way, they were believed to be possessed by demons.

People recognized physical illness but not mental illness. Physical illness might be able to be cured, and Jesus did cure many people. But mental illness was another thing altogether --- it was caused by demons and a way had to be found to exorcise those demons, to make them leave the possessed individual --- and no one really knew how to do that, but they tried.

Demonic possession stories appear throughout both the Old and New Testaments. In 1st Samuel 16:14 we read that King Saul was tormented by an evil spirit from the Lord.

Solomon is reported in 1st Kings as driving out demons and similar stories appear elsewhere in scripture.

Exorcists tried rituals, incantations and spells, potions and magical objects to drive out demons. Jesus was different. He didn't use any of these things. He just commanded the demons by his own authority and they immediately submitted.

Jesus asks the man his name. The demons answer "Legion," meaning that there were a lot of them. A legion of Roman soldiers numbered about 6000 men, so the name implied an incredible number of demons.

The possessed man had no name or identity. He was a total outcast. The people kept trying to catch him and chain him up. He was the worst of the worst in their eyes and here comes Jesus.

Jesus doesn't avoid the man. He comes and talks to him and orders the demons to leave him. He then orders the demons to enter a herd of swine that stampedes over a cliff and into the lake.

There you had the original "Bay of Pigs."

Yes, I know that it is a bad joke but it is symbolic, at least for Jews. Pigs were unclean animals. They were despised and a herd of pigs drowning in the lake had great meaning in the culture of the region. The Jewish Christians would have immediately understood and applauded the disposal of demons in this way.

But the problem in our story is that it took place not in Judea but in the region of the Gerasines, a gentile area. The pigs were owned by gentile swineherds. Those pigs were valuable to them and that is likely why the people rejected Jesus. His act of exorcising the man took away their livelihood, made them fearful, and they asked him to leave.

The man who had been cured and somehow clothed by Jesus asked to stay with him. Jesus told him to go home and to declare what God had done for him, and he did. We don't know how people reacted to the man's return.

What would you do or think if someone who you had rejected came back into the community? Would you accept him and listen to him or would your prejudices still be there? How do we learn to trust and accept someone who we previously rejected? Do we trust him or do we figuratively want to drive him off to live in the cemetery?

What about someone who committed a crime, was jailed, served his time, and came back? Would you trust him or her?

What about someone who was addicted to drugs or alcohol --- perhaps even a member of your own family? Would you willingly accept him or her back or would you hesitate?

In today's world, many people are afraid of immigrants, particularly those from the Near East. Could they be terrorists? Can we trust them? Should we trust them?

We all have demons --- fear of the past --- fear of the unknown --- fear of rejection. It goes on and on.

Jesus accepted everyone --- sinners, tax collectors, those who were demon possessed --- everyone.

Can we accept those who have changed? Those who are different? Those who are guilty by association? Can we do it?

Jesus would not have it any other way.

Amen.

A Story of Two Sinners
Luke 7:36-50

Our scripture reading is a story of two different kinds of sinners, a woman who presumably is a prostitute and a Pharisee.

To fully understand the story, you need to know how this woman could come in the first place without an invitation to what is obviously a banquet in honor of Jesus. It seems rather strange doesn't it?

Well the woman did not need an invitation because formal dinners in warm weather were generally held in an open courtyard of the houses of well-to-do people. The courtyards typically were square and there might be a garden or a fountain in them.

Whenever an honored guest was present, it was the custom for all kinds of people to come in to listen to what the guest had to say. These visitors would stand around the courtyard observing the meal and waiting to listen to the words of wisdom from the guest. That is why the woman could be present. She didn't break in or come uninvited. She was quite free to join the others who were present but no one expected her to do what she did.

You also need to understand that at a formal meal like this, the table was only a few inches high and guests sat in a reclining position, generally on a mat or low couch, with their legs extended.

The host of such an event always did three things when the honored guest arrived. He would touch the guest and give him a kiss of peace. William Barclay [1] points out that this was a sign of respect which would never be omitted in the case of a distinguished rabbi such as Jesus.

People back then did not wear closed shoes. They wore sandals and the roads were dusty, so the host would pour cool water over the feet of the guest to comfort and clean them. The host would also anoint the head of the honored guest with oil or incense. These things were demanded by good manners but, as the scripture reading tells us, they were not done.

So picture the scene --- the guests were reclined by the table resting on their left elbows so that their right hands were free. Their legs were stretched out pointing away from the table and their sandals had been removed. Thus any visitor standing around the table could be standing beside Jesus' feet, as the woman apparently was. That is the scene of the story as told by Luke.

Why would a Pharisee, of all people, invite Jesus as the honored guest at a banquet? If you think about it, that really is not very surprising. Jesus had a lot in common with the Pharisees. He loved the Law of Moses as much as they did and while he had issues with many Pharisees, that wasn't true for all of them. Nicodemus for example was a Pharisee who respected Jesus.

Even if Simon, the Pharisee in our story, had ulterior motives in inviting Jesus, Jesus couldn't well refuse the invitation. Jesus ate with tax collectors and sinners and to refuse an invitation from a noted Pharisee would, in the words of Fred Craddock [2], *"... have made him as guilty of reverse prejudice as some of those who discover in our zeal to right wrongs we develop prejudices against the prejudiced, a condition that places us in the camp of those we charge with standing in the way of God's reign on earth."*

Further, *"Houses in that culture were so constructed that the woman's entrance required no break-in, and since dining occurred in a reclining position, anointing Jesus' feet should not conjure up the image of a woman crawling around under a table."*

That is the setting and what the woman does is shocking. She lets down her hair, which a woman never does in public. She falls at Jesus' feet and begins to cry, her tears falling on his feet. She dries his feet with her hair and kisses his feet while anointing them with expensive ointment.

I suspect that Jesus knew who the woman was and might have talked to her previously on the streets. He knew her background and she knew who he was. The Zondervan Historical Commentary [3] suggests that she may have been so overwhelmed with the presence of Jesus and so grateful to him that she completely forgot her surroundings. In that culture kissing the feet indicates love. Jesus has forgiven her sins and she expresses her thankfulness with love.

The other sinner in this story, Simon the Pharisee, is aghast at the actions of the woman ignoring his own unforgivable actions of not extending to Jesus the simple courtesies that any host in that time would extend to an honored guest.

So, who is the greater sinner here --- the woman or the Pharisee?

Referring to the Pharisee's reaction to the actions of the

woman, in a sermon a few years ago the Rev. Edyth Pruitt at Fairview Presbyterian in Lenoir, NC said, *"Perhaps God's grace is always offensive unless you are the one receiving it."*

The Pharisee was offended. He didn't see the grace that had been extended to the woman nor did he understand that forgiveness produces love.

Each of us has been given this grace, this gift of forgiveness. Do we return this gift by expressing love for others? If we truly accept the grace that is freely given to us, we do.

Amen

1. William Barclay, The Gospel of Luke, rev. ed., The Westminster Press, Philadelphia, 1975.
2. Fred B. Craddock, Luke: Interpretation A Bible Commentary for Teaching and Preaching, John Knox Press, Louisville, 1990
3. Clinton E. Arnold, ed., Zondervan Illustrated Bible Backgrounds Commentary, Vol. 1, Zondervan, Grand Rapids, MI., 2002

We Are Number One, or Are We?
Mark 10:35-45

Go to any major sporting event and you will probably see the souvenir stands selling those big foam rubber "We are #1" hands and lots of people in the stands will be wearing them and waving them in the air whenever their team does something significant. Certainly a lot of them are in evidence on every Super Bowl Sunday.

If "We are #1" foam rubber hands had been available 2000 years ago, James and John might have bought them and waved them in the air in front of Jesus. It would be like Muhammad Ali who shouted out, "I am the greatest."

James and John clearly had big egos and were not shy about it. They thought that somehow or other they ranked above the other disciples.

After all, several times Jesus took them along with Peter to privately do things. He took them to the mountaintop, for example, when Jesus was transfigured.

They thought that they were the top team, #1, and didn't hesitate to make it known much to the consternation of the other disciples. It was rather like the key campaign aides to a Presidential candidate expecting choice positions in the candidate's cabinet if he or she is elected.

Jesus had just told the disciples for the third time that he would be killed and they still didn't understand.

"We are going up to Jerusalem and the Son of Man will be delivered over to the chief priests and the teachers of the law. They will condemn him and hand him over to the Gentiles, who will mock him and spit on him, flog him and kill him. Three days later he will rise." (NIV)

This was not going to be a picnic by any means and the Zebedee brothers couldn't see that at all.

They went to Jesus and said, *"Let one of us sit at your right and the other at your left in glory."*

James and John completely failed to understand Jesus according to William Barclay [1]. *"The amazing thing is not that this incident happened, but the time at which it happened. It is the juxtaposition of Jesus' most definite and detailed forecast of his death and this request that is staggering. It shows, as nothing else could, how little they understood what Jesus was saying to them. Words were powerless to rid them of the idea of a Messiah of earthly power and glory."*

Jesus tells them that they have no idea what they are asking for. *"Can you drink the cup I drink or be baptized with the baptism I am baptized with?"* Dawn Ottoni Wilhelm (2) said, *"... in the context of Jesus' impending death* [he] *more likely refers to the cup of bitterness and suffering. Jesus himself prefers to forgo this cup yet accepts it as necessary to fulfill God's will."*

What James and John were asking for, but didn't realize it, was to be like the two thieves who were crucified on the right hand and the left hand of Jesus. There was to be no earthly throne with chairs on each side for Jesus' trusted advisors.

The reference to his baptism *"... recalls the harsh beginning of Jesus' ministry and anticipates his death and the death of others who will suffer the baptism of blood when they give their lives for the sake of the gospel."* (2)

The other disciples are angered at the brothers Zebedee for trying to gain a position of power and Jesus responds, *"You know that those who are regarded as rulers of the Gentiles lord it over them, and their high officials exercise authority over them. Not so with you. Instead, whoever wants to become great among you must be your servant, and whoever wants to be first must be slave of all. For even the Son of Man did not come to be served, but to serve, and to give his life as a ransom for many."*

Jesus makes it abundantly clear that his ministry is to be the basis for the disciples' servant-ministry. *"Just as he came to serve, so are we to serve. Of equal importance, Jesus completely overturns all earthly perceptions of power, since he does not base his authority on lording it over others but on serving others."* (2)

Jesus is radically redefining what power is. Certainly leaders and persons in position of authority are necessary but Jesus is telling the disciples, and us, that no matter what we do, no matter what our profession is, no matter what position of authority we may hold, we are called to serve others by participating in the power of God's reign among us. Jesus is proposing a servanthood of all believers.

As his servants we are charged to serve others without seeking glory and personal gain. As Dawn Ottoni Wilhelm says, *"... the promise of Christ is that his cup is also our cup. As we drink of it and savor the sorrow and joy within it, we will taste his gift of freedom and salvation, in this world as in the world to come."*

Amen.

1. William Barclay, <u>The Gospel of Mark</u>, rev. ed., Westminster John Knox Press, Louisville, KY, 1975
2. Dawn Ottoni Wilhelm, <u>Preaching the Gospel of Mark</u>, Westminster John Knox Press, Louisville, KY, 2008

Mom and Dad Know Best, or Do They?
Acts 11:1-18

What is a good Jewish boy to do?

Saul of Tarsus, or Paul as he was later known, and Simon Peter were good Jewish boys. They grew up respecting what their parents taught them and were loathe to go against their Jewish teachings

Saul, of course, has his awakening on the road to Damascus where he encountered Jesus, and his life was changed forever. A militant oppressor of Jewish Christians became perhaps Christianity's greatest apostle.

Peter's life was turned around in a far different way. He was a Christian. He had accepted Christ. But he was also a Jew. His parents had taught him the Law of the Torah and that he had to respect them and observe the Law.

Following Jesus was not a problem for Peter. Jesus was the Messiah that the Jews had long awaited so to follow him fitted into what Peter had been taught but what happened to him in Caesarea changed everything.

Were it not for Saul's experience on the road to Damascus and Peter's experience in Caesarea, Christianity could well have remained as nothing more than an obscure sect of Judaism, but of course it didn't.

Both Saul and Peter learned that Mom and Dad did not always know best, and they learned it in startling ways.

Saul was a Pharisee, one of the keepers of Jewish law. Peter however was not a Jewish official. He was a humble fisherman who, probably unwillingly, became the leader of the early church. He had been taught what was clean and unclean

But Peter had a dream of a large sheet descending to the roof where he was sleeping in Caesarea. On it were *"all kinds of four-footed animals, as well as reptiles and birds."* Four-footed animals including pigs? Reptiles --- snakes and lizards? Birds --- eagles, vultures, buzzards? Quite possibly all of them.

Peter hears a voice saying, *"Get up, Peter. Kill and eat."* He refuses and hears the message two more times. He says, *"Surely not Lord! Nothing impure or unclean has even entered my mouth"* and the voice responds, *"Do not call anything impure that God has made clean."* (NIV)

Leviticus 11 says, in part, *"These are birds you are to regard as unclean and not eat ..."* and it lists many bird species. It also lists four-footed animals, animals which walk on all fours such as lizards and rats, and those that move along the ground such as snakes.

For Peter to do as the voice said was totally contrary to everything he had been taught.

Then, to make matters worse, three servants of a gentile, Cornelius, appeared asking for Peter and inviting him to come to Cornelius' home, which Peter does rather reluctantly.

Going to the home of a gentile, lodging there and eating with gentiles was also prohibited for a Jew. Gentiles were unclean and Jews were never to associate with them. Jews just didn't do that. Mom and Dad told them so.

In a way, that sort of quandary faces many Americans and has done so time and time again.

Irish immigrants were avoided. They were Catholics and Mom and Dad said to avoid them.

What about immigrants from Eastern Europe, like Lithuania where my grandparents came from. They were Catholics too. Stay away from them.

Then came two World Wars and Japanese and German immigrants and their descendants, even if they were upstanding law abiding citizens, were shunned. You can't have anything to do with these people --- no sir!

Then came people of Hispanic descent, Cubans, Guatemalans, and others but most particularly Mexicans. Watch out for them. You never know what they might do.

Now it is Muslims. We all know that they are terrorists. It doesn't matter if they were driven from their homes by ISIS and had friends and family members killed. You can't trust them. Mom and Dad say so.

History repeats itself over and over again and Mom and Dad don't seem to learn.

It took the Holy Spirit to go with Peter to Cornelius' home and to descend upon the people there and to bring those unclean gentiles to Christ.

Caesarea for Peter and Damascus for Paul were seminal moments which taught them what following Christ really means.

Paul went on to evangelize throughout the gentile world and Peter went back to Jerusalem to explain to the other disciples what he had experienced saying, *"If God gave them the same gift he gave us who believed in the Lord Jesus Christ, who was I to think that I could stand in God's way?"* The disciples said, *"So then even to Gentiles, God has granted repentance that leads to life."* (NIV).

God's grace extends to all of his people, even those Mom and Dad may have taught us to avoid --- the Irish, the Eastern Europeans, the Japanese and Germans, the Hispanics, the Syrians, everyone. Jesus told us to love our neighbors and all of them are our neighbors.

When are Christians everywhere truly going to do that? No sooner is one group accepted than another group seems to be excluded.

Many Christians are like the Torah-observing Jews in many ways but eventually we learn, as Paul and Peter did, that Christians are to be inclusive, not exclusive. But unfortunately with each succeeding generation, some moms and dads seem to forget that lesson and don't teach it to their children.

Love the Lord your God with all your heart, soul and mind, and love your neighbors as yourself, no matter where they come from, no matter what language they speak, and no matter what religion they practice.

That is what Jesus expects Christians to do.

Amen.

Turning 180 Degrees
Acts 10:34-48

Our scripture reading relates the seminal moment of evangelism --- Peter's acceptance of gentiles into the church. From that point forward the church grew and expanded throughout the known world.

Peter had done a 180 degree turn, a turn which later got him called on the carpet back in Jerusalem. It was a radical shift for Peter and for all of Christendom. Up to this point in time, the only Christians were Jews. The Jews believed that they, and only they, were God's chosen people. Those other people, gentiles, were unclean and were not deserving of God's grace. To the Jews, the gentiles were the scum of the earth. A Jew would never enter the home of a gentile, let alone eat with them. If a Jew ate with a gentile, he would become unclean himself. Gentiles were excluded because they were not of the Jewish line.

Does this kind of division sound familiar to you? It should because we live in a divided community, even today. Our churches are at odds with each other over who should and should not be members and who should serve as deacons, elders and pastors. Every denomination has this problem and, in each case, they forget about Peter and his transformation from being a kosher Jew to an apostle to everyone. Would that all churches remember and honor the words of Peter in Acts 10:34-35, *"I now realize how true it is that God does not show favoritism but accepts from every nation the one who fears him and does what is right."* (NIV).

In this context, what does it mean to fear God? It doesn't mean that one must be terrified of God. Rather it means that one must look at God with respect, reverence and awe. Quoting the Holman Illustrated Bible Dictionary [1], *"The proper attitude of believers toward God is often said to be respect, reverence or awe rather than fear ... Knowing that God's wrath has been satisfied in Christ relieves the believer from the fear of condemnation but not from accountability to a holy God ... To fear God is to have allegiance to Him and consequently to His instructions, thus affecting one's values, convictions and behavior ... So the fear of God expressed in humble submission and worship is essential to true wisdom."*

Peter was much like us today. He had his strong beliefs which he rigidly adhered to. To do otherwise would be heresy in his eyes.

Our churches similarly are divided by strong beliefs which they base on their interpretation of scripture, but other churches have a different interpretation. Roman Catholics believe that only unmarried men can be priests. That is their interpretation of scripture.

The Presbyterian Church in America believes that all clergy should be male, whether married or not.

In the Presbyterian Church USA anyone who is called by God can be a pastor.

These and many other differences have led to exclusion of one group or another in the various denominations because of the way that they interpret scripture. Yet, how can they dispute Peter's word that *"God does not show favoritism but accepts from every nation the one who fears him and does what is right."* It would be very hard to interpret that in any other way than inclusivity for everyone. Yet many Christian denominations are not inclusive. They do not recognize the revelation that came from Peter.

Peter was absolutely rigid in his beliefs. He was totally kosher. He was circumcised. He obeyed those 613 commandments to the letter but he had a vision, a vision of a sheet descending full of unclean animals, reptiles and birds. He is told to kill and eat and he refuses because these creatures are unclean. But a voice tells him, *"Do not call anything impure that God has made clean."*

Barbara Brown Taylor, an Episcopal priest, has written several books which I have read and enjoyed. In one of her books, *Bread of Angels*, she quotes the words of Peter to Cornelius that *"... God shows no partiality."*

Peter probably was surprised when these words came out of his mouth. He said this while *"... he was standing in the living room at the home of Cornelius ... Cornelius was one of the good guys, well regarded by the whole Jewish nation. He had even become a God-fearer, someone who believed in Israel's God, although as a Gentile he kept a certain distance ... he did not observe Jewish dietary laws, which was one of the main reasons Jews and Gentiles did not eat together."* (Barbara Brown Taylor).

Barbara Brown Taylor goes on to say, *"There were some Jews who believed Gentiles were just plain filthy, hopelessly immoral and prone to idolatry, but other Jews gave them the benefit of the doubt and lived with them in harmony. They simply could not eat together, that was all, because as hard as they tried, Gentiles might slip up and put some pork in the beans, or thicken a veal stew with milk".*

To put in perspective how important the dietary laws were to the Jews, to break those laws would be like us serving ham and Kentucky Bourbon, instead of bread and wine, when we celebrate the Lord's Supper. Why then do we use bread and wine, and not ham and whiskey or other some other food and drink?

It is because God, Jesus, told us to *"Do this in remembrance of me."* It is a given. It is not negotiable. That is what we Christians do.

For the Jews, their dietary laws were of similar importance. Observing those laws was what they did. Yet now, Peter realizes that those laws are not God's laws, that Christians are not bound by the old Mosaic Law but instead by the teachings of Christ. It is an incredible difference and for Peter it was a 180-degree change in his thinking.

Peter comes to Cornelius' home and finds a crowd of people, relatives and friends of Cornelius, all gentiles. He tells them that *"You are well aware that it is against our law for a Jew to associate with a Gentile or visit him."* (NIV). Peter says that at the door of the house.

Again quoting Barbara Brown Taylor, *"... I imagine some of them were crushed. Here they had waited for this great man whom Cornelius had told them so much about and he turned out to be just like all the rest, treating them as if they were dirty and he might catch something just by being in the room with them."*

Then Peter says the magic word, "But". God has shown him how wrong he was, that no one is profane or unclean and that he therefore came as requested and he enters the house.

Peter tells them of his vision. He literally opens the doors of Christianity to everyone, not just Jews.

His audience was probably stunned. Peter had turned 180 degrees. He tells them that Jesus is Lord of all, not just Jews and he begins to tell the story of Jesus, his ministry, his crucifixion and his resurrection.

Suddenly the Holy Spirit descends upon the crowd of gentiles and they begin speaking in tongues and praising God.

Peter says to friends who are with him, *"Surely no one can stand in the way of their being baptized with water. They have received the Holy Spirit just as we have"* (NIV) and he baptizes the entire group in the name of Jesus, the Christ.

Do you know anyone who is unclean? Do you believe that God's house is open only to certain kinds of people? I trust that the answer to these questions is a resounding **no!**

God's grace and salvation is open to everyone, even to people that we don't like all that much. God's church has wide open doors. Be evangelists. Spread that message to anyone who will listen.

Amen.

1. <u>Holman Illustrated Bible Dictionary</u>, Holman Bible Publishers, Nashville, 2003
2. Barbara Brown Taylor, <u>Bread of Angels</u>, Cowley Publications, Cambridge, MA, 1997

A Basket Case
Acts 9:19b-31

Saul received a direct call from Christ. He was chosen for a specific mission and he became Paul, Christianity's greatest evangelist.

It wasn't an easy task for Paul, not at all. On one side he had The Way, the early church, and its apostles and members questioning Paul's motives. They were afraid of him, understandably so. After all he had a reputation of seeking out Christians and having them arrested and at times killed. He witnessed the stoning of Stephen and supported it.

He had come to Damascus with letters of credit as an official agent of the Jewish faith and of the Sanhedrin, letters which authorized him to arrest Christians and extradite them to Jerusalem for trial.

The Christians knew that and were understandably wary of Paul. Wouldn't you be?

But Paul had been called a brother by Ananias, had been baptized, and had partaken of the Lord's Supper. Was he sincere or was this just a ploy to ingratiate himself to The Way and to infiltrate their ranks? Had he truly been converted to Christ or was he a spy? Clearly those worries would have been foremost in the minds of many of the Christians. Could they trust him?

But Paul had a sponsor --- a trusted disciple who spoke up for him --- Barnabas. Barnabas took Paul to Jerusalem to meet the apostles and told them the story of Paul's conversion and how he was now speaking out fearlessly in the name of Jesus in the synagogues of Damascus.

Paul had been going from synagogue to synagogue proclaiming that Jesus is the Son of God. Paul, according to William Willimon [1], was laying the theological groundwork to justify a mission to the gentiles but first Paul had a more immediate problem. He had to gain the trust of the disciples, both of the twelve and the later disciples.

The twelve *"... had to wait for the gift of the Spirit ... for the presence of the risen Christ ... before they could move out in power. Paul, who experienced the presence of the risen Christ (on the road to Damascus), must wait until his experience is validated by the Jerusalem apostles before he can move out with the assurance that his good news is apostolic." Paul first had to suffer in the name of Christ according to Acts 9:16.* The Lord said to Ananias, *"I will show him how much he must suffer for my name."* (NIV) Paul had to suffer, and suffer he did. He became a basket case.

He angered so many of the Jews in Damascus that they wanted to kill him. Damascus was a walled city and the Jews were watching the gates so that Paul could not escape the city. They formed a conspiracy to capture and kill Paul for what they believed was heresy. Paul had turned away from his teachings as a Pharisee and now was preaching that Jesus was the Son of God. Paul was doing the same things that Stephen had done --- he deserved to die as Stephen did. Paul couldn't get away. He was trapped in the city.

However, he had succeeded in gaining some followers. They put Paul in a basket and with ropes they lowered the basket through an opening high on the city wall and enabled Paul to escape. Paul literally was a basket case in more ways than one.

What exactly is a basket case? The phrase originally came from British slang during World War I. It referred then to people who had lost limbs in the war and could not get around on their own, but who had to be carried by others. In that sense Paul couldn't get out of Damascus on his own. He had to depend upon others to carry him out of the city, in this case in a basket lowered through an opening in the city wall.

The modern meaning of basket case also fits Paul in a way. Today, basket case means someone that is completely helpless or useless. Paul certainly wasn't useless but, while he was trapped in Damascus, he was helpless. He could do nothing for himself. He needed the Christian community to support him as they literally did while they lowered his basket down the outside of that wall. In that sense Paul was no different than any of us. We all need the community of the church for support in our lives. None of us can go it alone. If we try, we too become basket cases. Paul had to learn that lesson before the apostles in Jerusalem would accept him.

The apostles had elected Matthias to fill the vacancy in their numbers which was caused by Judas' betrayal and death. They all knew of Jesus' life but also needed to further experience his present power according to Willimon, and Paul was the example of that present power.

Paul's experiences on the road to Damascus were a dramatic example of Christ's power, an example occurring long after the resurrection, the ascension, and Pentecost. From that experience, Paul felt that he was now on a par with the apostles because he had independently received a realization of the truth of Christ.

However, to be accepted, he had to go to Jerusalem and convince the apostles. Paul couldn't operate independently any longer. He no longer was the zealous Pharisee heading out to Damascus on a one-man search and destroy mission. He had to be accepted and supported by the community of Christ, the church, if he was to succeed in a mission to the gentiles, his great mission to spread the Word beyond its original Jewish base.

Thanks to Barnabas who spoke up for him, the distrust of the disciples was overcome and Paul was off on his mission, his quest to bring the gentile world to Christ. Paul however quickly learned that discipleship often will involve suffering. He had been warned that he would suffer and it didn't take long for that to be confirmed. He avoids a murder attempt in Damascus, escaping in that basket. Grecian Jews also tried to kill him in Jerusalem. He is later stoned and left for dead in Lystra according to Acts 14:19. He is beaten and imprisoned on other occasions. He had to flee from Thessalonica. He seemed to go from one scrape to another, but he never wavered in his mission.

William Willimon said, *"Today, when the good news of Christ is often presented as the best deal a person ever had, the solution to all personal and economic problems, a good way for self-satisfied people to become even more satisfied, we do well to ponder the rough beginning of Paul's attempt to live out the good news. Discipleship, it would seem, is not necessarily the end of our problems but is more likely the beginning of problems which we would gladly have avoided if God had left us to our own devices. Before his conversion, Saul had the upper hand in life. He was in control, a persecutor of others. Now, after his encounter by Christ, he is a vessel (a basket if you will), an instrument in someone else's project, one persecuted rather than persecuting."*

Today, many TV and radio preachers, and many mega church pastors, preach what is called "prosperity gospel." Joel Osteen is probably the most significant example. Prosperity gospel preaching in effect says that if you give your life and resources to Christ, all of your troubles will go away --- your money problems, your medical problems, whatever your problems may be. You will become prosperous. You won't have a care in the world.

That form of evangelism works but only temporarily. Many people are drawn to the churches like Osteen's by promises like that but the promise is rarely fulfilled. Prosperity gospel is a revolving door. People who buy into it often become disillusioned and leave the church as fast as others come in.

Christ never promised us a life free of problems, a life free of economic woes. His promise is that we will find that in heaven, not here on earth.

We are frail sinful humans and the nature of being a human is that we do suffer. So long as we live on this earth, we need to expect that. Our reward will come later. In the meantime, we need the community of the faithful to support each other. That community is right here in church. That is the powerful message that all of us need to tell others if we are to build this congregation --- if we are to attract others to this community of faith.

Paul learned that the hard way. The gospel doesn't promise us prosperity. It promises salvation. That is a huge difference. That is the message of Paul. That is the message of Christ.

Thanks be to God.
Amen.

1. William H. Willimon, Acts: Interpretation, A Bible Commentary for Teaching and Preaching, John Knox Press, Louisville, 1973

God Speaks to Everyone
Acts 11:1-18

Paul received direct intervention from Jesus while on his way to Damascus to continue his persecution of the Christians. He was struck down, blinded, and then literally saw the Light and went on to become Christ's greatest apostle.

Paul was a Jew and had to overcome the resistance of the other apostles to him personally and also to his evangelizing the gentiles. Peter had a far bigger task. He had to overcome a life of obedience to 613 commandments from the old Mosaic Law --- commandments which excluded gentiles as unclean --- they ate forbidden foods, they were not circumcised, and they definitely were not part of God's chosen people. They were outsiders who the Jews had always shunned. Peter also had to see the Light and subsequently had to convert the other apostles accordingly. It was a traumatic time for Peter and it took a vision of unclean animals coming down to him on a sheet to awaken him. He was told to eat of these animals and replied, *"Nothing impure or unclean has ever entered my mouth."* In response, he three times heard the words, *"Do not call anything impure that God has made clean."* (NIV).

Then comes the request of Cornelius to tell him about Jesus and Peter finally abandons the kosher restrictions of Mosaic Law, enters Cornelius' home and brings Cornelius and his gentile friends to Christ.

But now Peter has to face the criticism of the other apostles and must convince them. He must bring them to the Light.

Up to this point in time, the Jews clearly understood that the Messiah had come to bring grace to the people of Israel, not to others. The apostles were all Jewish. Christ's followers were all Jewish. Jesus himself was Jewish. The Jews were God's chosen people. They believed that the Messiah was theirs and theirs alone. His grace was reserved for them. **But it wasn't.**

Jesus had shown time and time again that he accepted everyone, Jew or gentile, but that fact passed over the apostles' heads. They were limiting The Way, the early Christian church, to Jews and Jews alone.

That had to change and God had to directly intervene with

Paul and Peter to drive that point home. He had to get their attention, and indeed he did.

There was a huge number of people, profane people, unclean people in the eyes of the Jews, who were hungry for the message of Christ. Peter and Paul had to realize this. The gentiles wanted God to speak to them too and with the awakening of Paul and Peter, the floodgates started to open, but first Peter had to convince the other apostles and they in turn had to accept Paul.

Peter faced strong criticism from the apostles when they heard that he ate with gentiles, with unclean, uncircumcised men. His actions almost literally put Peter on trial. He had to justify his actions and, as our scripture passage from Acts 11 tells us, he did exactly that by relating the vision that he had received, by the fact that the Holy Spirit came to the gentiles, and that he had baptized them.

The Holy Spirit had come to the gentiles. Through the Holy Spirit, God had spoken to them. That was the clincher. The apostles then realized that God speaks to everyone and, as stated in Acts 11:18, *"... even to gentiles God has granted repentance that leads to life."* (NIV).

Back then, many gentiles were aware of Jesus and hungered for his grace. Once the apostles realized that God speaks to them too, and once they accepted Paul, their combined efforts began to encompass and expand throughout the then known world. The flood gates opened and the church grew. It grew because the church no longer excluded anyone.

Unfortunately, that rapid early growth has slowed to a crawl in present times and in this country and Western Europe, the church in fact has been shrinking. There is steady growth in the so-called Second and Third Worlds, the less affluent parts of the world --- Eastern Europe, Africa, South America and Asia. People there hunger for Christ and the church. Primarily through the work of missionaries, the church is rapidly growing in those areas. That is not true in North America and Western Europe.

Why isn't the church growing in the United States, and I mean Christianity in total, not just some denominations? Some individual churches are experiencing phenomenal growth for various reasons but they are the exception. On balance church membership in the United States is declining.

A few years ago, the Rev. Edyth Pruitt at the Fairview Presbyterian Church in Lenoir, NC, took a sabbatical leave to study this question and I, in fact, served as an interim pastor at Fairview until she returned.

When she did return, she highlighted three reasons that she had concluded were contributing to the problem.

First was the loss of people who had been hurt by the church and had dropped out. They hunger for the church but think that the church doesn't want them. It is rather analogous to the situation of the gentiles before their acceptance by the Jewish believers. Who are the people in this first group? Why did they leave?

Many left because of criticism from others in the church for any number of reasons. We Christians can be very judgmental. We criticize people for many reasons. We forget that Christ should be the judge of a person's actions and sins, not us. We shun people for their lifestyle, their appearance, their ethnic background, their manner of speaking, and more. We gossip and spread tales about others. We literally drive people away from the church.

An e-mail that I received said, *"Isn't it strange how difficult it is to learn a fact about God to share with others; but how easy it is to learn, understand, extend and repeat gossip?"* Sharing facts about God is what brings people to the church and keeps them here. Criticizing actions of others and gossiping drives people away --- often permanently.

The second group of people are those who are comfortable with their life. They have a good income, a nice home, good health and a loving family. They don't feel a need for God, yet they are often the strongest supporters and workers for mission activities --- food banks, youth groups, charities of all sorts. They are doing God's work but don't see the need for the church in their lives.

The third group are people with deep theological questions about spirituality. Their feelings about God are so deep that they have been pushed out of the church. They ask questions about why we do the things that we do. Why don't we do more? What is God really like? They aren't getting answers and wonder if their different way of thinking puts them outside of the people of God.

Churches, unintentionally or not, create barriers to people and those people fall into one of these three groups. How can we bring these people to the church, and avoid turning other people off?

The first group, those that have been hurt by the church

present the biggest hurdle. Many of them are bitter and resentful. If you know anyone like that, you need to talk to them in a careful and understanding way --- not a judgmental way. Listen to them. Find out what is of concern to them. Often the simple act of listening is all that it takes. Sometimes you can clarify their concerns and help them to feel better about the church. It may have been a simple misunderstanding that drove them away and you may be able to bring them back.

The second group, those who are content with their lot in life, may be the easiest group to reach. They are doing God's work in many cases but just don't see that through the church they can do even more. Ask them to participate in the mission activities of the church. Ask them to help out with a yard sale, the food pantry or some other project. That should be right up their alley and by helping out, they may come to realize that deep down, they too are Christians and can do much more through the church than they can accomplish individually.

Those with strong beliefs and unanswered questions shouldn't be ignored either. Ask them to sit down and tell you about themselves, what they are thinking, and what questions they may have in their minds. You may well bring them back simply by listening to them and you may well be able to answer at least a part of their questions.

Peter and Paul opened the floodgates by reaching out to everyone. The gates need to be reopened. Each of you can help, one person at a time, by seeking out their reasons for not being a part of the church and, depending upon which of the three groups they fall into, by responding appropriately. That is what evangelism is all about.

Thanks be to God.
Amen.

Table Fellowship
Luke 15:1-10

Our scripture reading is about salvation although it may not seem that way at first. Finding a lost sheep or a lost coin, how does that equate to salvation?

Sinners are lost and need to be found and the search for the lost sheep or the lost coin are emblematic of that.

But who is a sinner? What is a sin? I think that we all know the answers to those two questions --- we are all sinners and sin is anything we do that may be contrary to the will of God.

In the reading from Luke, and in many other places in the New Testament the Pharisees and scribes complain that Jesus is having table fellowship with tax collectors and sinners and thus he needs to be opposed.

Why did they complain about tax collectors separately from sinners? Weren't they sinners too? They were of course, but the Pharisees and scribes didn't see it that way. The tax collectors were agents of Rome and were considered to be just about the lowest form of life at the time because they were all considered to be corrupt. They had assigned quotas of tax money to collect and anything extra they would put into their own pockets. They were despised by everyone. Any person who associated with them was tarred with the same brush. It is no wonder that Jesus was criticized for his table fellowship with them.

But what about the other sinners? If the scribes and Pharisees did not consider themselves to be sinners, how did they decide exactly who a sinner was?

The answer is the 613 commandments in the Torah, the first five books of the Old Testament. The Pharisees and scribes rigorously observed the Torah and its commandments. If anyone did not do so, they were by definition sinners. The Pharisees referred to them as the "People of the Land."

William Barclay [1] said, "... *there was a complete barrier between the Pharisees and the People of the Land* [, the sinners]. *To marry a daughter of one of them was like exposing her bound and helpless to a lion. The Pharisaic regulations laid it down, 'when a man is one of the People of the Land, entrust no money to him, take no testimony from him, trust him with no secret, do not appoint him guardian of an orphan, do not make him the custodian of charitable funds, do not accompany him on a journey.' A Pharisee was forbidden to be a guest of any such man or to have him as a guest. He was even forbidden ... to have any business dealings with him."*

Of course, the Pharisees and scribes were not sin free, but in their minds they were. They strictly followed the letter of the Law of the Torah and bragged about it. They were exceptionally proud of their piety and of how they lived. Anyone who did not do as they did was a sinner in their eyes. We would call their attitude sinful, but they didn't of course.

Jesus said, *"... there will be more rejoicing in heaven over one sinner who repents than over ninety-nine righteous persons who do not need to repent."* (NIV)

Barclay [1] said, referring to the Pharisees, that they would have said, *"There will be joy in heaven over one sinner who is obliterated before God."*

The Pharisees and scribes were unforgiving and condemned Jesus for the fact that he was forgiving --- he forgave everyone who repented and in the ultimate sign of forgiveness gave his own life for the forgiveness of sin.

Have you ever embarrassed someone? If so, according to the Torah you are a sinner, a Person of the Land.

Are you superstitious? Do you eat bacon? Do you have a tattoo? Do you cut your hair? Do you eat raisins?

Doing any of these everyday things, and many, many more would have branded you as a sinner in the eyes of the scribes and Pharisees, but not in the eyes of Jesus.

The parables of the lost sheep and the lost coin, and the searches to find them, are illustrations of God's desire to find everyone who is lost, not to condemn them as might have happened with the Pharisees and scribes.

Breaking any of the 613 commandments in the Torah could conceivably have led to your being stoned to death. The Pharisees and scribes simply wrote off anyone who they considered to be a sinner. They didn't deserve forgiveness. They deserved nothing more than destruction.

For the shepherd with the lost sheep, he didn't write off the sheep which had strayed. It was his responsibility and he would search day and night to find the lost sheep and bring it back to the fold. He wouldn't condemn it for wandering off. He wouldn't give up hope and would rejoice when he found it, just as God rejoices when a sinner repents of his or her sin.

Similarly, the woman who searches for the lost coin on the straw-covered dirt floor of her home until she finds it is overjoyed just as God is overjoyed when a person who was lost to sin repents and comes to God.

Jesus doesn't have 613 commandments, many of which are trivial and meaningless. He only has two --- to love God and to love your neighbor.

When we seek to love God we receive his love in return. When we show love for our neighbor, God shows his love for us.

"Finding and restoring the lost gives pleasure to God as well as to all who are about God's business." (2)

The two parables *"... are not primarily calls to repentance. Sheep and coins can't repent ... These stories function as a disturbing response to the complaints of the Pharisees and scribes ... In answer to the complaint that Jesus has overstepped the boundaries in having table fellowship with sinners, the parables implicitly beckon the Pharisees and scribes to join him, to be a part of the searching, because God is a searching God."* (3)

We are also beckoned to table fellowship with our Lord. We too are sinners whom God is searching for.

Amen.

---

1. William Barclay, The Gospel of Luke, rev. ed., Westminster Press, Philadelphia, 1975.
2. Fred B. Craddock, Luke: Interpretation, A Bible Commentary for Teaching and Preaching, John Knox Press, Louisville, 1990.
3. Charles B. Cousar, et al, Texts for Preaching – Year C, Westminster John Knox Press, Louisville, 1994.

Get Up!
Acts 9:32-43

Our scripture passage this morning appears in Acts immediately after the account of Paul's conversion which I have talked about for the past three weeks but the events it relates actually happened earlier.

This passage is an abrupt transition to the evangelical work of Peter and somehow seems out of place and it is out of place in time. It is also a difficult passage to preach from and many pastors avoid it. One was quoted as saying, "I wouldn't touch that passage with a ten-foot pole." The reading consists of two stories, one of remarkable healing and one of someone being raised from the dead.

The reason some pastors avoid this text is because upon hearing this passage, some people immediately react with the question, "Why them? Why not my loved ones?"

Aeneas is suffering from a serious medical problem. He has been paralyzed for eight years. He was in hopeless condition and here comes Peter who says "Get up!" and Aeneas is cured. "Why doesn't God cure everyone who is seriously ill?" people ask.

Then Peter says "Get up!" to a woman who has died, Tabitha, and she sits up. She is brought back from the dead. Why doesn't God bring back a loved one who has died? Why Tabitha and not your father, your mother, a good friend, or someone else. Why, Why, Why?

Aeneas, get up! Tabitha, get up! Aeneas coom! Tabitha coom! And get up they do. Why them and not your loved one? That is an incredibly difficult question --- one which many pastors understandably want to avoid --- a question only God can fully answer, not anyone in a pulpit.

The Rev. Edyth Pruitt preached on this passage a number of years ago at the Fairview Presbyterian Church in Lenoir, NC. She told the story of two ministerial students in rural Alabama on a very hot summer day. They were doing evangelistic work. They walked up the path to an old and weather-beaten farm house, ran a gauntlet of barking dogs and screaming children and knocked on the screen door of the house. The woman of the house stopped her scrubbing over a tub and wash board, brushed her hair back, wiped the perspiration from her brow, and asked what they wanted. One of the students answered, "We would like to tell you how to obtain eternal life." The woman replied, "Thank you but I don't believe I could stand it."

There are numerous stories of remarkable healings in the scriptures and stories of people being resurrected. Lazarus was raised after four days. The daughter of a Roman official was raised. Crowds came to Jesus pleading for their health to be restored or for someone who had died to be raised, and it was done. Why then? Why not now?

In fact, it does happen today. Day after day you hear of someone who was miraculously cured of a disease. Doctors had given up hope but the person regains full health. We read of people who were clinically dead and came back to life. It happens but it is not God's plan for that to happen to everyone. His plan is for all of us to have eternal life with him, not eternal life of the kind we are experiencing today. We are humans. Humans suffer. Humans get ill. Humans die. We are not immortal. God didn't design humankind to be immortal. He has a far better plan for us.

Why then did Christ cure people and raise them from the dead? Why did Peter do it? There must have been a reason. After all, most of those people had little to look forward to in this life. Wouldn't they have been better off with God --- with eternal life?

Consider Tabitha. She was a widow. She was a Christian and was always helping the poor. Other widows were gathered around her body mourning. They showed Peter robes and clothing that Tabitha had made for them. Tabitha had a difficult life. She worked very hard and, as a widow in those days, she was pretty much ignored by society. She indeed had a hard life but the words, "Tabitha coom", "Tabitha, get up," brought her back to life. Wouldn't she have been better off with God? Why bring her back? Widows by definition back then were poor, very poor.

According to William Willimon [1], they were "... *on the bottom rung of society, without anyone to represent them, or protect them ... Her death has caused a crisis in the community. Now the most vulnerable ones (the other widows) have no one. Their coats and garments are tangible evidence of the life of Tabitha and what her death means for them. These widows do not concern themselves with questions of theology ... (they) are not interested in the consolations of a better world someday ... Tabitha is gone; how will they survive?*

"Surprise! Death will not have the final say ... (the) widows will not be left to perish. Tabitha is restored to them by Peter's bold word and act of solidarity. The name of Jesus Christ bears the same life-and-death-giving power as the creator of the whole universe ... the story says that the name belongs to widows and others who have no hope nor power except this name," the name of Jesus Christ.

God had a purpose in Tabitha's resurrection. She was needed by her community so God brought her back. Of course, she would not live forever, none of us will, but in this case it served God's purpose for her to live longer.

Christ's purpose in the many stories of healing and resurrection were presumably for similar reasons. One thing that is certain is that these miracles got people's attention and helped to bring many people to the faith. They also brought opposition to the work of Jesus, Peter, Paul and the other disciples from the Pharisees, the Sadducees and the Romans. They were disrupting the order of things and those in power don't like to have their world shaken up.

"Luke explains nothing in these stories, nor can you or I as interpreters" says Willimon. *"How God's agents wrench life from death in not something so trivial as to be explained. The stories can only be told and heard, asserted, inserted into life as they are thrust into the flow of Acts. It is not Peter who turns our history inside out but the story, the story which proclaims that our history is not closed and that there is someone ... there for the widows of the world."*

We can see why Tabitha was raised. Her job on earth was not complete. What about Aeneas? Why was he cured?

The answer is given in our scripture reading which tells us that *"All those who lived in Lydda and Sharon saw him and turned to the Lord."* (NIV). Aeneas was an example of what God can do and that example brought many others to the faith. We don't always know why others were cured or raised. God knows and it is not always for us to know.

Willimon goes on to say, *"These miraculous events are subversive to the present order, (that is the order of that time in history), for they announce a new age, an age where reality is not based upon rigid logic or cause effect circumstances but upon God's promise."* They are signs that, *"If it is by the finger of God that I cast out demons, then the kingdom of God has come upon you"* according to Luke 11:20 (NIV).

When these stories are told by Christians, by the church, *"... paralysis and death are rendered null and void."*

The stories have evangelistic and prophetic purpose. "Get up!' is said and nothing is ever quite the same again.

We don't have the power to evangelize as Peter did. We can't tell people to "Get up!" and cure them or raise them from the dead. But we do have power. That power lies in the grace and salvation offered to us by Christ with his crucifixion, resurrection and ascension.

Fr. Lopez Cessa said, *"Death has been conquered because Jesus died for us. For Christians, death is a sleep, and cemeteries are bedrooms. You wake up in the presence of God."*

We are humans. We get ill. We suffer and when God calls us, we die. But it doesn't end there. That is really where it begins. We just go to sleep and we do wake up. We wake up to eternal life in the presence of God." To evangelize we don't need to perform miracles as Jesus and Peter and the others did. We need to get up and tell others about the greatest of all miracles, the promise of grace, the promise that death is not the end. It is the beginning. We will wake up in the presence of God.

That is what those students wanted to tell that woman at the farmhouse in Alabama.

Amen.

---

1. William H. Willimon, <u>Acts: Interpretation, A Bible Commentary for Teaching and Preaching</u>, John Knox Press, Louisville, 1973

Insurmountable Odds
1 Samuel 17: 4-49

A shepherd boy, David, was anointed by Samuel to become the future king of Israel. Neither he nor his family had any idea why he had been anointed and it really did not have any immediate effect on Israel, King Saul, or David's family. Samuel knew why, but no one else other than God did.

How was it that a young shepherd boy could ever become king? The odds of that happening appeared to be insurmountable. He was very young, he had no connection in any way to the court of Saul, he was not a major figure in the army or the king's court, and he looked destined to live his whole life as a poor shepherd. So how did he get the chance to overcome these insurmountable odds?

If you recall the scripture about David's anointing, it concluded with *"...from that day on the Spirit of the Lord came upon David in power..."* and *"Now the Spirit of the Lord had departed from Saul, and an evil spirit from the Lord tormented him."* (NIV)

The Holy Spirit came to David and immediately left Saul. Saul had lost God's favor and David was destined by God to replace Saul. But how could David get into a position to do so? The answer was music. Saul was tormented after the Holy Spirit left him and he sought solace in music. He commanded his servants to find someone who could play the harp for him, one of his servants had seen David play the harp, told Saul about him, and David was brought to the court. David's music worked for Saul and whenever he heard David playing the harp, he would feel relieved. David had become the court musician. But how could a court musician, a young boy, ever become king. That would as ludicrous as the court jester becoming king, or one of us becoming President of the United States. It simply doesn't happen. Beating those insurmountable odds would be like winning the Powerball Lottery. Someone will win, but not you or I.

One of us could join a political party, actively work for the party, build a reputation and eventually get nominated and elected to some political office. Then after years of political work, standing for higher and higher offices, winning those elections, we might get nominated as President and possibly win. Our odds appear to be a lot better than David's. Things like ascending to a throne just don't happen, at least they don't unless there is something else supporting and driving the person --- something incredibly powerful --- something that David had --- the full support of God. Politicians today love to tell you how strong they are in their faith, they quote scripture as evidence, they make a public display of attending church, and they imply that God is behind their candidacy. They are blowing political smoke. It is doubtful if any of them has ever had Divine backing. But David did. Even so, something needed to happen to elevate David from being the court musician to a position of honor in the court. That something was the story of Goliath that was our rather long scripture passage this morning. The Lectionary suggested that only a portion of that passage be read but, to really understand the story, I felt that it was necessary not to leave anything out.

In that story, the Philistine army is facing the Israeli army and the Philistines have issued a challenge, rather than the two armies fighting to the death, let each army field a champion. The two champions would fight to the death. And the victor's army would take over the lands and peoples of the losing army. It almost seems civilized doesn't it? No massive battles would be fought, hundreds or thousands of deaths and injuries would be avoided, and one side would peacefully surrender to the other. Too good to be true? **It was**! The Philistine champion was a giant, Goliath of Gath. Goliath was a huge man clothed in many layers of armor. He terrified the Israelis and no one was brave enough to face up to him. The two armies stood facing each other for 40 days with Goliath's challenge being repeated each day.

Enter David who goes to the battlefront to bring food to three of his brothers who were serving in the Army, three brothers who were passed over when Samuel chose David to be anointed --- three brothers who were still most likely harboring some anger over that incident --- particularly Eliab, the eldest brother. Traditionally if a brother is to be anointed by a prophet, the honor goes to the eldest. Eliab had been passed over by Samuel, as had the second and third eldest, Abinadab and Shammah. Seven brothers had been passed over until Samuel reached the youngest, David.

When David goes to the battle lines with the food, he hears Goliath's challenge and is offended at the challenge to the army of Israel, the army of the living God, and the unwillingness of any one to take on the giant. He says he would fight Goliath and is laughed off by his older brothers. *"You, a mere boy, are going to fight that giant. It is ludicrous"* they told him but what David said was overheard and was told to Saul who called David to come to him.

David had the ultimate weapon, God, on his side. He told Saul that he had fought and killed a lion and a bear with God's help and that he would fight the Philistine because Goliath was defying the army of the living God, the army of Israel. David said *"The Lord who delivered me from the paw of the lion and the paw of the bear will deliver me from the hand of this Philistine."* (NIV). David's faith in God was so strong that he convinced Saul. No one else in the Israeli army would face Goliath but here was a mere boy, a boy of incredibly strong faith who was willing. Saul relented and told David to *"Go, and the Lord be with you."*

But it didn't happen quickly. Saul put his own armor on David and gave David his weapons but the result was almost comical --- a boy wearing the armor of the king, a large man, armor that was incredibly heavy as were the weapons. David probably could barely move wearing all that stuff. Small children often try to wear clothes of their parents – a hat which falls down over the child's face, shoes 10 sizes too large, pants which are longer than their legs, and so on. It is cute. They want to be like their parents and wear "grown up" clothes. Imagine if those shoes, hat and pants were made of iron a quarter of an inch thick. The child would fall over from the weight. That is what David felt like. He discarded the armor, the sword, the bow and arrows and went to face Goliath with only a sling and five stones.

Goliath is insulted by such an unworthy opponent. He vows to feed David's flesh to the birds and wild animals. David is not fazed by Goliath's boasts and says, *"This day the Lord will hand you over to me, and I'll strike you down and cut off your head. Today I will give the carcasses of the Philistine army to the birds of the air and the beasts of the earth, and the whole world will know that there is a God in Israel. All those gathered here will know that it is not by sword or spear that the Lord saves; for the battle is the Lord's, and he will give all of you into our hands."* (NIV)

I wonder if Goliath laughed at that. Here is the giant of a man, probably seven feet tall or so, covered over his entire body in armor, holding a sword, a spear and a javelin, facing a boy, a boy with only a few stones and a sling for weapons, or so the giant thought. But David had the ultimate weapon, God.

The enraged Philistine charges. David takes a stone and it hits Goliath in the only place on his body which is not protected by armor, his forehead. Armor has an opening for the wearer to be able to see out and a small part of the forehead is exposed by that slit. David was like a marksman with a rifle and a laser scope sight. He could toss a stone with similar accuracy to that of a shot from such a marksman and he was right on target. Goliath fell facedown onto the ground, David rushed forward, took the giant's sword and cut off his head.

David went on to become the leader of Saul's army and eventually, after Saul died, became king of Israel. David really became the father of Israel, the person from whom another King, Jesus of Nazareth was descended about 1000 years later.

What is the message of this story to all of us? It is one of the best known stories in the Old Testament. We grew up with this story and I am sure that some of you men, as boys pictured yourselves as David, as a person who could beat any odds to succeed if you were brave enough. Bravery really didn't have much to do with it for David. What mattered was faith in God – the faith that God would enable David to overcome seemingly insurmountable odds.

God is not going to give that sort of backing to most people, certainly not in our daily trials and tribulations but, if it is God's will, any of us can overcome insurmountable odds. In another sermon I talked about being in Saudi Arabia and hearing the phrase Muslims utter time and time again, Insha' Allah, meaning "if God is willing." I don't think that God controls much of what happens to any of us, day in and day out, year in and year out, but I do believe that when our faith is strong and when we face seemingly insurmountable odds, if the challenge facing us is important enough to our Lord, we can beat those insurmountable odds. Our efforts to build his church are not faced with insurmountable odds. Hopefully, we will be successful and the church will grow in membership and in further service to our Lord, Insha' Allah.
Amen.

A House Divided
Mark 3:20-25

"If a kingdom is divided against itself, that kingdom cannot stand. And if a house is divided against itself, that house cannot stand."

Abraham Lincoln quoted these words of Jesus in his famous *House Divided* speech which led to his being nominated over Stephen A. Douglas in 1858 as the Republican Party's nominee for US Senate. The speech was referring, of course, to slavery and the divisions which it was causing in the country. Lincoln was defeated in that election but two years later was elected as President of the United States. Before he took office, the house divided political climate of the country resulted in seven Southern States seceding from the Union and only a month after his inauguration, the Civil War began. Lincoln inherited the house divided --- he didn't cause it --- but it was up to him to reunite the country.

After the crucifixion, the apostles, notably Paul, also had to struggle with a house divided, in this case the fledgling Christian church. Some of the apostles wanted only circumcised Jews in the Church. Gentiles were not welcome. God fearers, those gentiles who accepted Christ and agreed to be circumcised, were accepted somewhat reluctantly.

Paul evangelized the gentiles and did not see the need for them to observe the Jewish laws, thus causing a sharp division with Peter. That split fortunately was resolved in due course but other divisions kept cropping up, not the least of which was the tendency of some people in the churches to hold onto pagan ways or to otherwise break from the teachings of Christ. Notable in this regard, of course, was the church at Corinth, to which Paul had to direct major attention to keep redirecting them back to the teachings of Christ and to correct their misunderstandings.

Adding to all of this came persecution from the Romans, and it really was not until the time of Constantine that the Church really spread in unity.

Then came the Reformation in the 16th century which split the Christian house with the Protestant movement breaking away from the Roman Catholic church. That division has never been healed. Catholics and Protestants still struggle in various parts of the world, sometimes violently, as had been the case in Northern Ireland for many years.

Protestantism itself has never been united. From the start there were the Lutherans, mostly in Germany and Scandinavia, and the reformed churches, notably in Switzerland, the Netherlands and Scotland. Many other smaller denominations came into existence then. Scotland, of course, was where the Presbyterian Church has its roots.

These various denominations spread around the world, and most of them split and divided again and again, including the Presbyterian Church in this country.

The big split was, like the country, over slavery when the former Northern and Southern Presbyterian Churches were formed. It took over 100 years until they reunited as the Presbyterian Church USA, the PCUSA, in 1983. Even then, it was not a full reunion as several other Presbyterian dominations continued to exist, notably the Presbyterian Church in America, the PCA.

The hopes and prayers that the PCUSA would reunify most, if not all, Presbyterians were short lived. One issue after another continued to bedevil all churches, not just the PCUSA, and splits and divisions seemingly are occurring throughout Protestantism almost daily. There are probably 100 or more Protestant denominations now --- Pentecostal, Fundamentalist, Baptist, Lutheran, Methodists, and on and on.

Those churches which call themselves Presbyterian include the PCUSA, the PCA, the Evangelical Presbyterian Church, the Associate Reformed Presbyterian Church, the Cumberland Presbyterian Church, and others.

Denomination after denomination has split over integration, ordination of women, sexual orientation, divorce, social outreach, liberal versus conservative politics, and more.

Within the PCUSA, some churches are struggling with the question of whether or not they should remain as a part of the PCUSA or withdraw to another denomination. At Presbytery meetings and at the PCUSA's General Assembly gatherings this issue is always a hot topic of discussion.

As a pastor, the failure of Protestants, and specifically Presbyterians, to resolve these disagreements pains me deeply. Paul and Peter in the early church faced an incredible task and with the guidance of the Holy Spirit were successful. Why can't we do the same? I don't have an answer but I can reflect upon some of the causes of these divisions. In my mind, these divisions, at least within the various Presbyterian denominations, come not from the teachings of Christ but from human failure. Satan undoubtedly has his hand in it too.

These divisions have happened due to things which Jesus would have been appalled about. Splits happened over women being pastors or elders. Why? Jesus had many women among his disciples, yet some churches and denominations still resist women in leadership positions.

The Rev. Shannon Kershner, pastor at Fourth Presbyterian Church in Chicago, gave a powerful sermon at a meeting of the Presbytery of Western North Carolina which addressed this problem. She said, *"...it was only 106 years ago on a fresh whisper of the Spirit, that Northern Presbyterians decided, 'Well, perhaps God can call a woman to be a deacon.' And it was only 82 years ago on a fresh whisper of the Spirit that Presbyterians decided, 'Well, perhaps God can call women to be elders.' And it was only 56 years ago on a fresh whisper of the Spirit that Presbyterians said, 'Well, I guess God can even call a woman to be a minister, Lord help us.'"* It took nearly 2000 years for Presbyterians to listen to the whispers of the Spirit, and that was not all Presbyterians. The PCUSA, yes, but not the PCA and other denominations.

How do sinners, that is, all of us, fit in? Jesus loved and accepted all sinners --- tax collectors, prostitutes, thieves, anyone! What about homosexuals? How do they fit in? Are they included? That question is a major source of current divisions within the PCUSA. In 1st Corinthians 6:9-11 Paul refers to homosexuality, adultery, drunkenness, slander, and other sins and says about them, *"You were washed, you were sanctified, you were justified in the name of the Lord Jesus Christ and by the Spirit of our God."* (NIV). Christ died for the forgiveness of all sinners who accept him as Lord and Savior. Why then are churches so divided over one form of sin to the exclusion of other forms of sin?

What about race? Jesus did not distinguish people by race, yet race has been a major cause of church divisions and still is in some churches. Why?

Many of these problems exist because, instead of listening to the Holy Spirit, churches and denominations have divided because of "proof texting" the scriptures. Proof texting is taking a few words out of context from the scriptures and using those words to justify actions. Proof texting should never be done. All of scripture should be read and understood in its full context. Our politicians proof text all of the time in their ads. You see it on TV day in and day out. Pull a few words out of an opponent's speech, quote them out of context, and suggest that the opponent stands for something other than what he or she really stands for.

A favorite of proof texters are Paul's letters to the Corinthians. In them, Paul is addressing very specific problems of the Church at Corinth and is not suggesting that what he says should apply to all Christians. He meant his comments only for Corinth and the special circumstances of that Church --- not for all Christians everywhere for all time. The context is important, yet denomination after denomination ignores that fact.

I could go on and on but I hope that you see my point. Those who call themselves Christians have accepted Jesus Christ as Lord and Savior. We needn't judge others. Christ will do that. It is His job, not ours.

If all churches would listen to the Holy Spirit and stick to the words of Christ and what he taught us, we would no longer have a house divided. We would have a house united in love, in the everlasting love of God.

Our scripture passage ends with these words of Jesus: *"Here are my mother and my brothers! Whoever does God's will be my brother and sister and mother."* (NIV). Jesus included everyone, no matter what their lot in life, no matter what their sins were. If all churches would learn to do that, we wouldn't have a house divided.

What are you going to do to help heal the centuries of wounds that Christians have caused? Isn't it time that we put aside the non-issues which have divided the church in the past? Isn't it time that we opened our arms wide to anyone and everyone who will accept Christ? If we did that, if all Christians did that, we would achieve what Jesus clearly desired all Christians to do from the time he gave his life on that cross on a hill called Golgotha.

Amen.

Seeing: The Last Miracle
Mark 10:46-52

Mark's Gospel was the first of the four gospels to be written down and actually is the basis for both Matthew's and Luke's gospels but Mark's manner of writing is different from the others.

It in great measure concentrates on telling of the miracles performed by Jesus --- driving out demons, healing lepers, healing a paralytic, raising the dead, curing blindness, feeding the thousands, and more.

The final miracle happened when Jesus was on his way to Jerusalem with his disciples to face what he knew would be his crucifixion. Three times he has told the disciples what is going to happen but they refuse to accept it --- they have a big blind spot which they can't overcome, as is the case with all of us. It is convenient to have blind spots to block out what we don't want to see. We can avoid a lot of unpleasantness that way.

Our scripture reading is the story of healing a blind beggar, Bartimaeus. Bartimaeus was a nobody, a nothing in the eyes of the people of Jericho. He was ignored by everyone. He was the kind of person people could walk right past and not see. People were as blind to him as he was to the world.

In those days, people were often given names which told who they were, and the names would occasionally be changed to reflect changes in their situation. I suspect that such was the case with Bartimaeus, I really doubt that Bartimaeus was the name his parents gave him --- it more likely is a name he was called when he became blind and had to resort to begging to survive.

Bartimaeus quite literally means "son of poverty" or "son of the unclean." Another translation is "son of filth." Can you relate to that? Son of filth? That certainly is not a name given him at birth. It is more likely that as a blind beggar he was dirty, he wasn't clean, and the name was given to him by those who saw him.

So here we have this despised man sitting by the roadside --- a man ignored by the crowd --- a man who was virtually unseen in the blind spot of those around him.

But Bartimaeus was a stubborn man. He shouted out, *"Jesus, Son of David, have mercy on me!"* when he heard people say that

Jesus was coming by. The people told him to be quiet. They tried to shut him up but he persisted. *"Son of David, have mercy on me!"* (NIV).

Jesus heard him and called to him. Bartimaeus threw off his dirty cloak, possibly the only possession he had. He sprang up and went to Jesus.

Jesus asked, *"What do you want me to do for you?"* and the blind man said, *"My teacher, let me see again."*

"Let me see again" tells us a lot. Bartimaeus was not born blind. Somehow he had lost his sight --- perhaps due to an accident --- perhaps due to a disease such as macular degeneration --- perhaps due to cataracts --- or to something else.

In any event Bartimaeus knew what sight was. He was familiar with it and he desperately wanted to see again.

Can you imagine knowing the beauty of a flower, a bluebird, mountains and hills, forests, the faces of our loved ones and then losing the ability to see? It is hard to imagine something more depressing. Bartimaeus knew what sight was and he was desperate to get it back just as you or I would be.

We have sight, but we don't see everything around us, not at all. In life we have many blind spots. We block out things that we don't want to see, things that are unpleasant to think about or things that we have forgotten.

As Christians we have, at least in theory, committed ourselves to follow Jesus, but do we always do that? Following Jesus is hard to do because at times he leads us to places we don't want to see, places we don't want to visit.

The Rev. Edyth Pruitt at Fairview Presbyterian Church in Lenoir, NC, in a sermon that she gave several years ago on today's scripture passage, contrasted a parent walking in the woods with a child. The adult focuses on following the path. The child's eyes wander and see much that the parent misses --- a flower blossom, an insect, a bright stone, a chipmunk, and so on. The parent is oblivious to these things and walks right by them. The parent is full of blind spots, but the child is not.

Similarly, we don't see things in ourselves. We don't see things that we do, or don't do, that are not right. We have blind spots and at times we love to be blind.

When I was writing this message, I took time out to read an article by Ed Cyzewski entitled "The Supreme Court Just Gave American Evangelicals a Gift."

(http://edcyzewski.com/2015/06/26/the-supreme-court-just-gave-american-evangelicals-a-gift/)

It was written a few days after the Court's ruling on same sex marriage.

The premise of the article was, no matter what your personal opinion is of the Supreme Court ruling, so much energy, time and money was spent on fighting against same sex marriage that Christians fighting it had tended to become blind to much greater concerns of far more importance to the faith. Those greater concerns were and are ones that Jesus pointed to --- *"The most basic aspects of human dignity: food, shelter, clothing, justice and sickness ---*

"For I was hungry and you gave me something to eat,
I was thirsty and you gave me something to drink,
I was a stranger and you invited me in,
I needed clothes and you clothed me,
I was sick and you looked after me,
I was in prison and you came to visit me."

Mr. Cyzewski said, *"We can disagree all day on same sex marriage* [and] *most likely will continue to disagree about this issue for 20 years ... However, there's no denying that millions of people around the world are suffering significantly, and Jesus wants us to focus our energies on serving them. If there ever was a group of people who should* [care] *about children dying of hunger, deeply wounded people suffering in prison, and thousands upon thousands of refugees fleeing unprecedented violence in the Middle East it should be* [Christians]..."

He goes on to say that we aren't called to fight against someone. Doing so puts us into a big blind spot, one in which we overlook Jesus' true call to us, which is to fight for those who are suffering in the most basic ways. We need to focus on the hard things in life, not the flowers, the bluebirds and the mountains --- but on poverty, illness, oppression, hunger, and more.

As Rev. Pruitt said, blind spots tell us that we don't need to change. Faith tells us something different --- even if it leads to Jerusalem.

Jesus, Son of David, have mercy on us. Let us see.
Amen.

Don't Overestimate Yourself
Mark 9:38-50

We all know the story of how the disciples squabbled among themselves as to which of them was the greatest (Mark 9:30-37). They were acting like children and Jesus called them to task saying *"Anyone who wants to be first must be the very last, and the servant of all."* (NIV).

Our scripture reading from Mark again shows how the disciples tended to overestimate themselves.

It opens with John complaining to Jesus that an exorcist, one who is not a disciple of Jesus, is casting out demons in Jesus' name.

In Biblical times, demonic possession was a common belief. People believed that mental illness and even some physical illnesses were caused by demons, evil spirits. The belief was that in order to get rid of a demon one needed to know about an even more powerful spirit and to command that the evil spirit come out of the person in the name of the more powerful spirit. Demons were believed to be unable to resist the might of the more powerful name.

Here we had a man who was not a follower of Jesus using Jesus' name to exorcise evil spirits. The disciples saw that he had been successful and they objected.

Psychologically if a mentally ill person encountered such an exorcist and believed that Jesus does have the power to cure him, by using Jesus' name the exorcist might well be successful in effecting a cure but the problem was, in the disciples' eyes, that he was not a follower of Christ. He shouldn't be using Jesus' name. That was something that only his followers, that is the disciples themselves, should be allowed to do.

Jesus came right back at the disciples telling them that there was nothing wrong in the exorcist doing things in his name. To the contrary, it reinforced Jesus' authority.

Joshua made the same sort of complaint to Moses (Numbers 11:26-30) to stop unauthorized prophets. Moses replied, *"Are you jealous for my sake? I wish that all the Lord's people were prophets and the Lord would put his Spirit in them."* (NIV)

In Jesus case, he told the disciples, *"...whoever is not against us is for us."*

The disciples seemed to think that they somehow or other were superior to others. They were overestimating themselves. The exorcist was successful and they had forgotten that they were not always successful. Only a short time earlier they had tried to cure a boy, were unsuccessful, and had to bring him to Jesus, who did cure him (Mark 9:14-29).

William Barclay [1] comments that today's scripture reading is a lesson in tolerance that everyone needs to learn. Everyone has his or her own thoughts and has the right to think things out and come to their own conclusions and beliefs. That is a right that we should respect and not condemn things that we don't understand.

Alfred Lord Tennyson said that, *"God fulfills himself in many ways."*

Cervantes said, *"Many are the roads by which God carries his own to heaven."*

Quoting Barclay [1], *"This world is round, and two people can get to precisely the same destination by starting out in precisely opposite directions. All roads, if we pursue them long enough lead to God. It is a fearful thing for any person or any church to think that they have a monopoly on salvation."* The disciples certainly did not have such a monopoly although they may have thought they did.

As Jesus said to the disciples, *"Truly I tell you, anyone who gives you a cup of water in my name because you belong to the Messiah will certainly not lose their reward."* (NIV).

The scripture reading goes on to talk about, *"... these little ones --- those who believe in me ..."* and those who cause them to stumble.

The reference to "little ones" is not necessarily to children. In its broadest sense of meaning it refers to new believers and Jesus is admonishing the disciples to reflect on their own lifestyles and their ministry. Are they doing anything which might serve as a stumbling block for the new believers?

The exorcist, although he was not a follower, was curing people in the name of Jesus. He was creating new believers. To stop him would create a stumbling block.

Jesus states that it would be better for someone who creates a stumbling block for a believer to be tied to a millstone and thrown into the sea to drown or to lose a hand or a foot. The examples are graphic and include reference to being thrown into hell and to being salted with fire if a person causes someone to stumble in their faith.

The references to drowning or cutting off a limb are not meant to be literal but must be taken seriously. Lamar Williamson, Jr. [2] said, *"The surpassing value of entering the Kingdom of God makes every other good expendable."*

The reference to being thrown into hell does not mean sulfur and brimstone and an evil figure with horns and carrying a pitchfork. It really is an illusion to being thrown out with the garbage. The word translated from the Greek as "hell" is "Gehenna" referring to the valley of Ben Hinnom just outside of Jerusalem. At one time idol worshippers offered child sacrifices there. Later it became the town garbage dump which was kept on fire to prevent pestilence. So being sent to hell was a vivid image of one being worthless, being of little more value than garbage.

The scripture reading has four major points [3]

1. *"Not being one of us"* is not an acceptable criterion for determining who is not a Christian.
2. Hospitality is to be practiced freely.
3. New converts must be accorded special care and consideration. Causing a new convert to stumble is a grave sin.
4. The life of a disciple must be morally earnest inasmuch as our behavior has eternal consequences.

In her book "Preaching the Gospel of Mark" [4], Dawn Wilhelm said in referring to the last portion of our scripture reading, *"...images of salty disciples and refining fires compel us to consider anew what is distinctive and enduring about the Christian faith. Even with low-salt diets and microwave ovens, no one doubts the essential value of salt and fire for sustaining life ... Salt refers to the enduring quality of faith and service. Fire can refer not only to the fire of hell but the fire of heaven when God stirs within us a passion for serving others."*

It is not up to us to decide who is or is not a Christian or to set our own criteria for who can be a Christian. It is up to us to show hospitality to all and to nurture and care for those who are seeking Jesus. Whatever we do must demonstrate faith and service and show our will to serve Christ through serving others.

Amen.

1. William Barclay, The Gospel of Mark, rev. ed., Westminster John Knox Press, Louisville, KY, 1975 (Quotes have been rephrased to make them gender neutral).

2. Lamar Williamson, Jr., <u>Mark: Interpretation, A Bible Commentary for Teaching and Preaching</u>, John Knox Press, Louisville, 1983
3. Fred B. Craddock, et al, <u>Preaching Through the Christian Year - Year B</u>, Trinity Press International, Harrisburg, PA 1993.
4. Dawn Ottoni Wilhelm, <u>Preaching the Gospel of Mark</u>, Westminster John Knox Press, Louisville, KY 2008